THE BEST CONVERSATION YOU EVER HAD

4 Steps To Fruitful Conversations With Anyone

DARIUS BROWN

Your Conversation Coach

"The Best Conversation You Ever Had"

ISBN: 979-8-9884858-4-1

Published by R.E.A.P Connections LLC.
www.getyourconversationcoach.com

TABLE OF CONTENTS

Introduction

Welcome to "The Best Conversation You Ever Had Workbook," your comprehensive resource for cultivating fruitful conversations and improving communication skills. Effective communication is more critical than ever in today's fast-paced world, as it serves as the foundation for successful collaborations, career advancement, and meaningful personal connections. However, communication problems can extend beyond the workplace, infiltrating our personal lives and complicating our interactions.

Consider the following statistics:

- According to research, communication issues are common in professional and personal settings. An American Psychological Association (APA) study states that ineffective communication is the top workplace stressor for 65% of employees.

- Workplace conflicts, which are frequently the result of communication breakdowns, have serious consequences. According to a Society for Human Resource Management (SHRM) report, 25% of employees have considered quitting their jobs due to workplace conflicts, resulting in lower productivity and employee engagement.

- External factors, such as unresolved conflicts in personal relationships, can infiltrate other aspects of life, including the workplace. According to the Impact of Personal Relationships on Communication in the Workplace study published in the Journal of Organizational Behavior, employees with unresolved conflicts have more difficulty communicating effectively with colleagues and supervisors, resulting in strained working relationships and lower productivity.

Personal relationship issues can significantly impact overall well-being and communication skills. According to the American Institute of Stress, 80% of respondents reported stress-related symptoms caused by personal relationship issues, resulting in difficulties in communication, concentration, and overall quality of life.

These figures demonstrate how widespread communication issues are and how they affect both work and personal lives.

"The Best Conversation You Ever Had Workbook" considers the effects of these outside factors and gives you the tools and techniques to deal with these challenges, leading to better communication and personal and professional relationships.

Based on the ideas in my first book, "The Best Conversation You've Ever Had with Yourself," this workbook goes a step further by giving you tools and techniques to use intentionality in your conversations with others. You can unlock a new level of connection and significance by approaching conversations with intention, a sincere desire to connect, and a commitment to producing positive outcomes.

Throughout this workbook, we'll dive into the REAP Conversation Method: Rapport Building, Engaging Questions, Active Listening, and Proper Response Tools. These four pillars will guide you in creating conversations that go beyond small talk and connect on a deeper level. Just as a farmer carefully tends to the soil, sowing seeds and nourishing them, you'll learn how to build rapport, ask meaningful questions, listen actively, and respond in a way that fosters understanding and growth.

We'll also explore the three soils of conversation: Shallow Soil Conversations, Thorny Soil Conversations, and Fruitful Soil Conversations. Each soil represents a different level of depth and impact in our conversations.

Rapport Building is like preparing the soil, creating a foundation of trust and understanding. Engaging Questions are the seeds we plant, igniting curiosity and fostering meaningful dialogue. Active Listening is like watering the seeds, nurturing their growth with an attentive presence. And Proper Response Tools are the tools we use to harvest the fruit of fruitful conversations, responding in a way that fosters understanding and growth.

Are you ready to level up your communication skills? Let's embark on this journey together, exploring practical strategies, engaging in reflective exercises, and cultivating the skills needed to have the best conversations of your life. Get ready to transform how you connect, one conversation at a time.

Let's dive in and unlock the power of intentional conversations, growing fruitful conversations that nurture understanding, connection, and personal growth.

Chapter 1: Intentionality in Conversations

Have you ever had a conversation where you walked away feeling unsatisfied or misunderstood? The lack of intentionality played a role. Intentionality is more than just the words we choose; it's about the energy we bring, the purpose we set, and the desired fruit we want to produce. When we approach our conversations with clear intentions, we set the stage for fruitful and meaningful exchanges.

Throughout this chapter, we'll explore the concept of intentionality and its profound impact on our communication. Whether you seek to improve your professional communication skills or enhance your relationships, this chapter will equip you with the tools to do just that.

The Power of Intention

The Role of Intentionality:

We engage in countless conversations in our daily lives. Some are brief and superficial, while others are deep and meaningful. Have you ever stopped to consider intentionality's role in these interactions?

Intentionality is the driving force behind every conversation we have. It is the conscious decision to approach a conversation with a purpose, a desired outcome, and a genuine interest in connecting with the other person. When we engage with intentionality, we bring focus and clarity to our conversations, transforming them from mere exchanges of words into powerful and impactful experiences.

But why is intentionality so crucial in conversations? It goes beyond simply exchanging information or filling the air with words. Intentionality shapes the outcome and quality of our interactions, influencing the level of connection, understanding, and mutual respect we can achieve with others.

Intentional conversations enable us to navigate complex topics gracefully and sensitively, leading to more effective conflict resolution and problem-solving.

Recognizing Lack of Intention:

In pursuing intentional conversations, we must know the signs and challenges of unintentional interactions. Lack of intention can hinder effective communication and create barriers to meaningful connection. Let's explore some common pitfalls and challenges that arise when intentionality is absent in our conversations.

One of the critical challenges of unintentional conversations is the need for more direction and purpose. Without clear intentions, conversations can meander aimlessly, lacking focus and clarity. Unintentionality can result in a lack of transparency, communication, and a missed opportunity to connect on a deeper level. Recognizing this lack of intention allows us to course-correct and bring purpose into our conversations.

Another challenge is the risk of superficiality. When we engage in conversations without intention, we often stay on the surface, discussing trivial topics and missing out on the opportunity to delve into more meaningful discussions. Unintentionality can prevent us from truly understanding and connecting with others on a deeper level. By recognizing this lack of intention, we can consciously go beyond small talk and explore more substantial topics.

Lastly, unintentional conversations need more authenticity and genuineness. When we don't approach a conversation with clear intentions, we may unintentionally put up a facade, saying what we think others want to hear or hiding our true thoughts and emotions, creating a barrier to authentic connection and hindering trust-building. Recognizing this lack of intention allows us to be more vulnerable, open, and genuine in our conversations, fostering more profound and meaningful connections.

Noticing Your Intention:

It's incredible how much our intentions shape the direction and quality of our interactions. So, please consider why you're engaging in a conversation and what you hope to achieve through it.

Developing self-awareness is critical here. It's like turning on the inner spotlight and becoming aware of your thoughts, emotions, and motives when you enter a conversation. By being aware of your intentions, you can make conscious choices about how you want to appear in the interaction.

Imagine you have a meeting with a colleague to discuss a project. Before diving in, pause for a moment and notice your intention. Are you seeking to collaborate, understand their perspective, or promote your ideas? Awareness of your intention helps you approach the conversation with clarity and purpose.

Aligning Your Intentions:

Now, let's talk about aligning your intentions with desired outcomes. Picture this: Your intentions are like the compass that guides your conversation. Suppose you intend to listen to and understand the other person. It sets the stage for a more open and empathetic exchange. On the other hand, if you intend to prove yourself right or win an argument, it can create a defensive and combative atmosphere.

Imagine you're conversing with a team member with a different opinion than yours. If you intend to understand their perspective and find common ground, you're more likely to have a productive discussion. However, if you want to convince them without considering their viewpoint, it can lead to conflict and hinder collaboration.

By aligning your intentions with desired outcomes, you increase your chances of having a positive and constructive conversation. It helps you stay focused on the purpose of the interaction and ensures that your words and actions align with your goals.

Having a clear intention is crucial before engaging in any conversation. However, I would argue that the conversation you have with yourself is even more significant. It shapes your intentions and determines whether you can follow through on them. While we may have the best of intentions, lacking a clear understanding of our inner selves can lead to unexpected outcomes during our interactions, hindering our ability to fulfill those positive intentions. Let's delve into how an unhealthy inner dialogue can cause disconnection within a conversation.

For example, imagine you have a genuine intention to resolve a conflict with a coworker. However, if you haven't addressed your own emotions and insecurities beforehand, you might inadvertently project your frustrations onto the other person during the conversation. This could result in further misunderstandings and escalate the conflict, ultimately undermining your initial intention to find a resolution.

By acknowledging the importance of our inner conversation and taking the time to understand ourselves, we can foster better communication and ensure that our intentions align with our actions, leading to more meaningful and fruitful conversations.

Let's explore things to look out for internally resulting in your unhealthy inner conversation getting in the way of your best intentions.

How an Unhealthy Inner Conversation Causes Disconnection

1. Overcoming Fear and Resistance:

Let's tackle a vital aspect: fear and resistance in conversations. These barriers can appear in various ways, like the fear of judgment or rejection or the resistance to vulnerability. They can hold us back from fully engaging and expressing ourselves authentically.

To overcome these challenges, we need to understand where they come from. Often, fear and resistance stem from past experiences, societal expectations, or simply a lack of self-confidence. By identifying and acknowledging these fears, we can start addressing them and finding strategies to overcome them.

When considering workplace dynamics and communication, it is essential to acknowledge common fears and barriers that can impede effective interaction. Let's explore some examples and delve deeper into how these fears can create a culture of silence, hindering collaboration and innovation.

One prevalent fear is the fear of speaking up in meetings. Many individuals may hesitate to share their thoughts or ideas due to a fear of judgment or a lack of confidence in their contributions. This fear can lead to a culture where only a few dominant voices are heard, while valuable insights from others remain untapped. As a result, the organization misses out on diverse perspectives and innovative solutions that could have emerged through open and inclusive discussions.

Another fear is the fear of giving or receiving feedback. Constructive feedback is crucial for personal and professional growth, yet individuals may be hesitant to provide honest feedback out of concern for hurting others' feelings or facing potential backlash. Similarly, the fear of receiving feedback can stem from a fear of criticism or negative evaluation. When feedback is avoided or sugar-coated, it hampers individual development and inhibits a culture of continuous improvement within the workplace.

Resistance to change and new ideas is yet another barrier to effective communication. Change can be unsettling for many, and the fear of the unknown or the potential disruption it may cause can lead to resistance. When employees are resistant to change, it becomes challenging to introduce new initiatives or embrace innovative approaches. This fear-based resistance stifles creativity and impedes progress, preventing the organization from adapting to evolving circumstances and staying competitive.

In a bit, we will address these communication problems and fears because the goal is to make sure you have organizations that can foster a culture that encourages open dialogue, psychological safety, and a growth mindset.

2. Stretched Mental Capacity:

Our minds are incredible, but they can only handle so much. When juggling various aspects of our lives, like personal and professional responsibilities, it's easy to become overwhelmed with thoughts, emotions, and unresolved issues. This mental overload can have a significant impact on our conversations.

Imagine a day when you have a million things on your mind: deadlines to meet, tasks to complete, and personal matters to attend to. In such moments, it's natural for our mental capacity to be stretched thin. We may engage in shallow conversations, where we only exchange basic information, or engage in small talk without connecting.

Have you ever had a conversation where you couldn't entirely focus or engage because your mind was preoccupied with other things? That's the result of stretched mental capacity. These shallow conversations need more depth and substance, preventing us from building meaningful relationships and hindering our professional growth.

Another consequence of mental overload is rushed conversations. When our minds are racing, we may struggle to actively listen to and understand others. We might find ourselves interrupting, jumping to conclusions, or simply not giving our full attention. It can lead to miscommunication and missed opportunities for collaboration.

Imagine a scenario where you're discussing a project with a colleague, but a hundred other things consume your mind. It becomes challenging to truly listen and understand their ideas, resulting in misunderstandings and ineffective teamwork.

By recognizing the impact of mental overload on our conversations, we can take proactive steps to create mental space and cultivate self-awareness. It's about figuring out how to declutter our minds, prioritize our thoughts, and create the space necessary to engage in more meaningful conversations.

Each interaction and situation we encounter elicits emotional responses within us. When these emotions are left unaddressed, they can accumulate and lead to what I call emotional obesity, where our emotional well-being becomes burdened and overwhelmed. To ensure our inner clarity and resilience, it is crucial to proactively manage and process the emotions accompanying our daily experiences. By doing so, we expand our emotional capacity, enabling us to engage in the conversations we desire with greater effectiveness and authenticity.

I'm going to show you how to create more mental capacity shortly.

3. Hearing Through Trauma Filters:

Our past experiences shape who we are and how we perceive the world. They imprint on our minds and hearts and can significantly influence our communication with others. These experiences can act as filters, distorting how we hear and interpret the words and actions of those around us.

Think about it: Have you ever felt intensely emotional about a seemingly innocent remark? Sometimes, certain words might remind us of past traumas or negative experiences, making us react defensively or with heightened sensitivity. "Hearing through trauma filters" is what this is.

When we listen through these filters, our communication becomes distorted, and our relationships can suffer. Innocent remarks will become misunderstood, leading to thorny conversations filled with defensiveness, conflict, and an inability to understand and empathize with others.

Imagine you've experienced a failure in the past that left you feeling inadequate. During a team meeting, someone innocently points out a mistake you made. Because of the influence of your past experiences, you may hear it as a personal attack instead of constructive feedback, creating a tense atmosphere and impeding collaboration and growth.

It's essential to recognize and address these trauma filters for healthier conversations. By becoming aware of our triggers and understanding how they affect our communication, we can start to untangle the knots and create space for more open and authentic conversations.

Recognizing trauma filters allows us to approach conversations with greater empathy and understanding. We can learn to separate the present moment from the past experiences that shaped our filters. It's crucial to cultivate self-awareness and practice self-compassion as we navigate our interactions.

The next section will explore practical strategies and techniques to clear mental space, cultivate healthier inner conversations that create meaningful relationships.

The 4A Process:

Now, let's explore a powerful tool that can help you overcome the barriers to fruitful intentional conversations caused by unhealthy inner conversation. It's called the 4A Process, and it serves as a solution to overcoming fear and resistance, recognizing and overcoming your trauma filters, and clearing your mental space. Let's dive in.

The 4A Process is like a compass that guides you through your inner conversations, enabling you to navigate the challenges and create more fruitful connections the 4A Process is a series of questions and prompts that help you overcome your fears is wrong with filters and clearing mental space so that you can align yourself with the intention you had when you wanted to have that conversation. The void process is comprised of four words that start with the letter A. Let's explore how each component of this process ties into the previous topics we discussed:

First, we have Awareness. This component emphasizes developing self-awareness in your inner conversations. By becoming more aware of your thoughts, emotions, and communication patterns, you can recognize the intentions behind your words and actions. Remember when we discussed the importance of aligning your intentions with desired outcomes? Awareness plays a vital role in that process. By understanding your intentions, you can ensure that your conversations are authentic, purposeful, and aligned with desired results.

The second step is to Address it. This step encourages you to actively engage with your thoughts and emotions, addressing them rather than suppressing or ignoring them. Remember when we explored the impact of capacity overload and how it leads to shallow conversations and challenges in active listening? Addressing it also leads to clearing up your trauma filters so that you're not hearing the wrong way during your conversations with colleagues, team members or team meetings. Addressing inner dialogue is crucial to creating mental space and overcoming those challenges. Acknowledging and engaging with your thoughts and emotions creates an opportunity for deeper understanding, reflection, and growth.

Next, we have to Accept it. This step invites you to acknowledge and embrace where you are after addressing your emotions and embrace your thoughts and emotions without judgment or resistance. This includes acknowledging the limiting beliefs that lead you to your current situation, accepting the reality of your situation and forgiving yourself. It ties into our previous discussion on hearing through trauma filters. When you recognize and accept the influence of past experiences on your communication, you can create a non-judgmental space within yourself. By accepting your thoughts and emotions, you cultivate self-compassion and a supportive inner environment. This acceptance allows you to break free from distorted communication patterns and foster healthier conversations.

Finally, we come to the step Accelerate. This step is about transforming negative inner conversations into empowering ones by intentionally moving forward by faith, choosing to believe something different and taking action steps rooted in a place of healing. Remember when we discussed the impact of trauma filters on communication? In the acceleration stage, you actively work on recognizing and addressing those filters. By cultivating positive affirmations, self-belief, and empowering narratives, you can overcome the limitations imposed by past experiences. This positive shift in your inner conversation empowers you to have more meaningful conversations, build trust, and create genuine connections.

The 4A Process serves as a holistic solution to overcoming fear and resistance, noticing your intentions, and clearing your mental space. It's a robust framework that enables you to navigate your inner conversations and enhance your interpersonal interactions. Incorporating the 4A Process into your daily life can transform your communication style and create more meaningful connections with others.

For detailed guidance on each component of the 4A Process, I recommend referring to my previous book,"The Best Conversation You Ever Had With Yourself" workbook. It provides valuable resources to support you on your journey of self-discovery and growth.

The next chapter will dive into The Three Soils of Conversation. We will explore the different types of conversation soil that can either hinder or nurture meaningful connections. We will examine the characteristics of the Shallow Soil, the Thorny Soil, and the Fruitful Soil and understand how they impact our relationships and communication.

Chapter 2: The Three Soils of Conversation

In this chapter, we will explore the understanding of conversation through the lens of the Three Soils: Shallow Ground, Thorny Conversations, and Fruitful Conversations. Get ready to dig deeper and uncover the dynamics of each soil type and its relationship to intentionality.

Shallow Soil Conversations:

Picture a garden with a shallow layer of soil. This shallow layer is synonymous with conversations that need more depth to create meaningful connections. Intentionality is often lacking in the Shallow Soil Conversation, and conversations revolve around superficial topics and small talk. These conversations may leave us unfulfilled, as they rarely lead to genuine connections or profound understanding

Shallow Soil Conversations sound like this:

Small talk about weather and current events: In these conversations, the focus remains on surface-level topics such as the weather, sports, or popular news. The interaction lacks depth and fails to explore meaningful subject matter.

Example: "Nice weather we're having today, isn't it? Did you catch the game last night?"

Exchanging basic information: These conversations involve sharing basic details about oneself, such as names, occupations, or where one is from. While it establishes initial rapport, it often doesn't progress beyond these introductory details.

Example: "Hi, I'm Sarah. I work in marketing. How about you?"

Superficial topics and gossip: Conversations revolve around shallow topics like celebrity gossip, television shows, or material possessions. They provide momentary entertainment but lack substance or significance.

Example: "Did you see that viral video? It was so funny! And did you hear about the latest drama with that celebrity?"

Polite, but disconnected exchanges: These conversations maintain a polite tone but lack authentic engagement or emotional connection. People may exchange pleasantries without delving deeper into each other's experiences or feelings.

Example: "Good morning! How are you?" "I'm fine, thank you. How about you?" "Doing well, thanks."

While these conversations serve a purpose, they rarely create lasting connections or cultivate deeper relationships. We need intentionality in these conversations to explore meaningful topics and connect more deeply.

Thorny Soil Conversations:

Let's discuss Thorny Soil Conversations and how they can be challenging and conflict-ridden, similar to a garden overgrown with thorny bushes. These conversations arise not because they are inherently bad, but rather because they contain seeds of potential conflict. Despite our initial intentions to cultivate fruitful discussions, these conversations can become entangled in thorns, stifling their positive potential. Thorny Conversations often emerge when intentionality is absent from our communication, resulting in heated arguments, misunderstandings, and persistent disagreements that strain relationships and impede genuine understanding.

Consider a family gathering where sensitive topics arise, such as political beliefs or past conflicts. Without intentionality, the conversation can quickly turn thorny. Family members may engage in heated debates, speaking over one another, and becoming emotionally charged. The lack of intentionality in their words and actions prevents a productive and empathetic exchange. As a result, relationships may become strained, and understanding between family members may remain elusive.

Fruitful Soil Conversations:

Let's step into the most rewarding part of the garden: Fruitful Soil Conversations. Here, intentionality takes root and blossoms, nurturing deep and meaningful connections. Just as a garden yields abundant fruits, intentional conversations bear the fruits of trust, understanding, and genuine connection. Every word, gesture, and response in these conversations is purposeful and contributes to a mutually enriching dialogue. It's not only because everything flows perfectly in the conversation; rather, it's because the seeds of discord are crushed in the soil, creating an environment where conflicts are properly addressed, and true intentions strive to know the other person's mind, experiences, and emotions in a safe and empathetic space.

Imagine engaging in a collaborative team meeting where every member feels encouraged to share their ideas and perspectives. In Fruitful Conversations, intentionality guides our actions and words. We actively listen to one another, empathize, and seek to understand different viewpoints. These conversations foster a culture of respect, trust, and open communication, leading to innovative solutions and strengthened teamwork.

By embracing intentionality and addressing unhealthy inner dialogues, we transcend the limitations of Shallow Ground and navigate through the challenges of Thorny Soil Conversations. Intentionality allows us to foster authentic, meaningful, and transformative connections. It empowers us to actively engage with others, understand their experiences, and create a safe and nurturing communication environment where fruitful conversations can flourish.

Conclusion:

In this chapter, we explored the Three Soils of Conversation: Shallow Ground, Thorny Conversations, and Fruitful Conversations. We discovered how intentionality plays a crucial role in shaping the depth and quality of our interactions.

We learned that conversations in Shallow Ground need more depth and need to create meaningful connections. Without intentionality, these conversations often revolve around superficial topics and small talk, leaving us wanting more substantial engagement.

On the other hand, Thorny Conversations can be challenging and filled with conflicts. When intentionality is lacking, misunderstandings and disagreements arise, straining relationships and hindering genuine understanding.

In contrast, Fruitful Conversations bloom when intentionality takes root. These purposeful conversations create a space for deep connections and mutual understanding. We can nurture authentic and transformative communication by actively listening, empathizing, and seeking to understand others.

Now that we know the importance of intentionality in conversations, we are ready to dive into the next chapter, exploring the REAP Conversation Method. This robust framework comprises four key components: Rapport Building, Engaging Questions, Active Listening, and Proper Responses.

Rapport Building sets the foundation for meaningful conversations by establishing connections and building trust with others. Engaging Questions help us delve deeper into topics, encouraging thoughtful and open dialogue. Active Listening allows us to fully understand and absorb what others say, fostering genuine understanding and empathy. Proper Responses involve responding effectively and appropriately to contribute to the flow and depth of the conversation.

Through the REAP Conversation Method, we will gain practical techniques and strategies to enhance our communication skills and create more intentional and impactful conversations. It will guide us in developing more potent connections, fostering understanding, and building deeper relationships with others.

But before we move forward to the next chapter, let's take a moment to explore and identify your typical conversation soil.

What's Your Normal Conversation Soil?

Instructions:

Please answer the following questions based on your self-assessment. Be honest and choose the option that best reflects your typical behavior in workplace conversations. This exercise aims to help you understand your conversation style, so avoid overthinking your answers.

1. When engaging in conversations at work, I tend to:

a. Express my opinions confidently and assertively.
b. Listen actively and encourage others to share their thoughts before expressing my own.
c. Keep the conversation brief and focus on essential information.

2. In challenging or conflicting situations, I am more likely to:

a. Defend my position and strive to prove my point.
b. Listen attentively and try to understand the other person's perspective before responding.
c. Seek compromise and find common ground to resolve the issue.

3. When giving feedback to a colleague, I:

a. Provide direct and honest feedback, even if it may be uncomfortable or critical.
b. Ask open-ended questions to help the person reflect on their performance and growth areas.
c. Highlight both strengths and areas for improvement in a balanced manner.

4. How do you typically handle disagreements or differing opinions in team discussions?

a. Advocate for my perspective and engage in persuasive arguments.
b. Encourage open dialogue, respect diverse viewpoints, and seek a collaborative solution.
c. Look for areas of agreement and try to find a compromise.

5. When faced with a complex problem, I:

a. Take charge and provide clear directions for problem-solving.
b. Collaborate with others, leverage their expertise, and jointly find a solution.
c. I prefer to gather information independently and come up with my approach.

6. In conversations, I am most focused on:

a. Achieving specific outcomes and driving results.
b. Building relationships, understanding others, and fostering a positive and inclusive environment.
c. Conveying my ideas and making sure my point is understood.

Scoring:

Count the times you selected each option (a, b, c). The option with the highest count represents your more frequent conversations at work.

Interpretation:

- **If you have mainly selected option (a):** your conversation style tends to lean towards Thorny Conversations, where you are assertive and prioritize defending your point of view. Reflect on ways to balance assertiveness with empathy and collaboration in your communication approach.

- **If you have mainly selected option (b):** Your conversation style reflects Fruitful Conversations, emphasizing active listening, understanding others, and fostering a collaborative environment. Continue nurturing this approach and seeking opportunities to enhance your communication skills further.

- **If you have mainly selected option (c):** Your conversation style tends to lean towards Shallow Ground Conversations, where you focus on brief exchanges and seek compromise. Consider exploring ways to deepen your connections and engage in meaningful and impactful dialogue.

Remember, this assessment provides a general indication of your conversation style and is not an exhaustive evaluation. Use the results as a starting point for self-reflection and personal growth.

Recognizing areas for improvement is the first step toward developing more vital workplace communication skills. As we progress through this workbook, we will explore strategies and techniques to enhance your communication abilities and foster a more productive and positive work environment.

Introduction to the REAP Conversation Method

In the previous chapters, we've explored the diverse nature of conversations and their profound impact on our relationships. Now, we will delve into a dynamic framework known as the REAP Conversation Method. It's like an agricultural or farming manual that guides us through cultivating fruitful conversations.

Just as a farmer meticulously prepares the soil, plants the seeds, nurtures the growth, and eventually reaps the delectable fruits, the REAP Conversation Method guides us through a systematic process to yield the best outcomes in our conversations. Each step within this method builds upon the previous one, emphasizing the significance of approaching our conversations with attentiveness and intentionality.

The first is Rapport. Think of it as preparing the soil before planting the seeds. Like a farmer who ensures the soil is fertile and ready for growth, establishing rapport sets the foundation for meaningful and open dialogue. It's all about building trust, creating a safe space, and fostering a genuine connection with the other person. When rapport is strong, the conversation has a solid foundation to flourish.

Next up are engaging questions, like planting quality seeds in the soil of the conversation. By asking thoughtful and thought-provoking questions, we can stimulate deeper insights, encourage reflection, and uncover valuable information. These questions catalyze growth and exploration, creating fertile ground for meaningful dialogue.

Active listening is the third step. It's like watering the seeds and watching them grow. When you practice active listening skills, you give the speaker your full attention, understanding, and empathy. You nourish the conversation by absorbing the essence of what's said. Like watering plants, active listening ensures that the seeds of conversation are well nurtured and given the space to flourish.

Lastly, we have proper responses about harvesting the fruit we've grown with the right tools. By responding effectively and appropriately to the information shared, we bring clarity, address concerns or questions, and move the conversation forward positively.

It's like carefully harvesting the crops that have been grown. With proper responses, we reap the rewards of effective communication and further enhance the connection.

By following the REAP Conversation Method and embracing the parallels with the farming process, we gain a comprehensive framework to navigate conversations with skill and intention. It allows us to create a place where good conversations can happen, which leads to stronger relationships, better teamwork, and more professional success.

Let's kick things off with the first step of the REAP Conversation Method: Rapport.

Chapter 3: Rapport Building - Preparing the Soil

Have you ever met someone who connects with others effortlessly? It's like they have a magic touch in sparking conversations anywhere they go. They can create an atmosphere of trust and understanding in minutes. Their secret lies in their ability to build rapport.

Knowing how to spark connections is necessary to make a great impression on people. Building rapport is the foundation of most connections, whether you're talking to someone you know well or someone you've just met. It's like preparing the soil of someone's mind for a deeper conversation, like the "Fruitful Conversations" we talked about earlier. You need to lay the groundwork before you can have those meaningful exchanges.

Building rapport requires intentionality. You must know why you want to build rapport with a person and what you hope to achieve through the connection. Having a clear intention gives your conversation a sense of purpose and direction. It helps guide you toward the outcomes you desire.

But here's the thing, building rapport is not about simply agreeing with everything someone says or showering them with compliments. It's much deeper than that. Think of it as building a bridge between two people. The first step is creating an environment where the other person feels comfortable sharing their thoughts and feelings. You want to create a safe space where they can open up. Now, you can start bridging the gap between you and the other person.

Building rapport is a powerful tool to have in your communication toolbox. The sooner you start practicing it, the better you'll become at it. Eventually, people will come to expect that genuine connection from you.

Rapport is all about moving beyond surface-level conversations. It's about transitioning from discussing the superficial "what" to understanding the "who" behind it. Small talk is fine, but it's only scratching the surface.

So, let's explore some practical strategies for building rapport with anyone you meet. We'll go beyond the surface-level "what" and discover the "who" behind it. Let's dive in!

How do you build Rapport?

There are two ways to establish trust with someone you know or don't know.

The two most important ways to build rapport are to:

1. Look for commonalities and ask an open-ended question.
2. Give a compliment, and then ask open-ended questions.

1. Pointing Out a Commonality + Open-Ended Question

Building rapport is all about finding that spark of connection, something you both have in common that brings you closer. It could be as simple as discovering shared interests in your day-to-day life, like your hobbies, travel experiences, or even the type of car you drive. These little things can become the starting point for deeper conversations and help establish a sense of trust. By genuinely seeking out these connections and showing an interest in what makes the other person tick, you create a friendly atmosphere where meaningful exchanges can flourish.

By attentively observing others, you can identify shared traits and experiences that serve as a bridge between your intention and building connections. Pay close attention to their speech, shared information, background, attire, or even subtle details like scent. These observations help prepare their mind for a meaningful conversation, setting the stage for deeper connections and fruitful interactions.

Here's an example of combining a commonality with an open-ended question:

Commonality: You both enjoy cooking.

Example Question: "I heard you mention your passion for cooking. What's your favorite recipe that you love to prepare?"

By pointing out their shared interest in cooking and asking an open-ended question about their favorite recipe, you create an opportunity for them to share their culinary experiences and engage in a deeper conversation. This approach allows for a more meaningful exchange of ideas and helps build a stronger connection, even in a work setting. Remember to actively listen to their response and show genuine interest in their cooking journey.

2. Give a Compliment + Open-Ended Question

Giving compliments and asking open-ended questions are powerful tools for building rapport. When giving compliments, it is crucial to express genuine appreciation and recognition, creating a positive impression. Thoughtful compliments have a profound impact on our well-being and can uplift our souls. Additionally, when complimenting someone's appearance or possessions, it is important to focus on the person rather than the item itself. Avoid generic compliments and instead offer specific compliments that highlight their unique qualities.

The Power of Genuine Compliments

Studies show that compliments activate the same brain area as receiving cash. Genuine compliments have a profound impact on our well-being and can uplift our souls.

Here are things to keep in mind when complimenting others.

Complimenting Something Tangible

When complimenting someone's appearance or possessions, focus on them rather than the item itself.

For example, instead of generic compliment like "I like your shirt"

say something like "That shirt looks great on you."

It focuses on the person and makes them feel seen!

Here's another example:

Compliment: Congratulations on your recent promotion.

What's Wrong with this Compliment?

This compliment focuses on the achievement but lacks personal connection and specificity.

The Correct Way to Compliment

Compliment: "Your attention to detail, willingness to listen and provide insights, and proficiency in your work are truly commendable. It's evident why you received this promotion. Congratulations!"

Open Ended Question: "What's the most fulfilling part about your new role so far?"

While it may seem natural to congratulate someone on their recent promotion, it is essential to go beyond the achievement itself. Instead, focus on their attention to detail, willingness to listen and provide insights, and proficiency in their work.

I can already hear some of you, as you're reading the book, thinking that it would require knowing the person well to give such a detailed compliment. However, I want to challenge that thought process. There are certain commonalities that are prevalent in our world when it comes to promotions. While there may be situations where favoritism plays a role, in most cases, a promotion indicates that the individual has been excelling in their work. They have demonstrated their commitment by working long hours, going above and beyond their job role, and staying dedicated to their teams. By recognizing these commonalities, you can tap into the deeper journey they took to achieve the promotion and offer a compliment that goes beyond the promotion itself. This approach allows you to prepare the soil of their mind for a fruitful conversation.

Closing Tips for Building Rapport

Before we move on to the next step, let's go over some vital closing tips for building rapport:

1. Be genuine and specific with your compliments. When giving compliments, it's essential to be sincere and focus on particular qualities or characteristics. Generic compliments can come across as insincere or superficial, whereas genuine compliments create a stronger connection and build trust. So, make sure your compliments are heartfelt and tailored to the individual.

2. Transition from the "WHAT" to the "WHO" behind the "WHAT": One of the keys to building deeper connections is moving beyond surface-level conversations. Shift your focus from discussing external events or facts (the "WHAT") to exploring the personal motivations, perspectives, and values (the "WHO") behind those events. This shift allows for more meaningful and engaging conversations that foster genuine connection and understanding.

Building rapport is like preparing the soil and planting the seeds for fruitful conversations. The seed you intend to plant represents the foundation for the next step: asking engaging questions. In the REAP Conversation Method, this is the "E." It's crucial to ensure that the seed you plant is healthy and capable of fostering meaningful dialogue.

Engaging questions are not your typical everyday questions. Engaging questions spark deeper conversations and elicit insightful responses. These questions go beyond surface-level information and tap into the person's thoughts, emotions, and experiences.

Think of engaging questions as seeds that have the potential to grow into meaningful conversations. When you ask these questions, you create an environment where the other person feels comfortable opening up and sharing more about themselves.

So, are you ready to dive into the meaning of engaging questions and unlock their true power?

But before we explore that further, let's take a moment to put your newfound knowledge to the test and practice what you've learned.

End of Chapter Quiz:

1. What is the primary goal of building rapport in communication?

A) To avoid misunderstandings
B) To establish trust and deeper connections with the other person
C) To prove your knowledge on a subject
D) To gain power over the other person

2. What are some effective strategies for building rapport with someone?

A) Giving compliments and asking open-ended questions
B) Only talking about shared interests
C) Making assumptions about the person's background
D) Criticizing the person's work

3. How does building rapport relate to the REAP Conversation Method of communication?

A) It is the last step in the method
B) It is unrelated to the method.
C) It is the first step in the method.
D) It is the second step in the method and involves preparing the soil of the person's mind for deeper conversation

4. Why is it important to transition from talking about the "WHAT" to the "WHO" when building rapport?

A) It helps to avoid awkward silences in the conversation.
B) It allows for a deeper and more meaningful conversation.

C) It allows you to show off your knowledge on a subject
D) It helps to establish dominance in the conversation

5. What are some characteristics of effective compliments when building rapport?

A) They should be general and non-specific
B) They should be about the person's physical appearance
C) They should be genuine and specific
D) They should be backhanded compliments to maintain control

Answer Key:

1. Answer: B) To establish trust and deeper connections with the other person
2. Answer: A) Giving compliments and asking open-ended questions
3. Answer: D) It is the second step in the method and involves preparing the soil of the person's mind for deeper conversation
4. Answer: B) It allows for a deeper, more meaningful conversation
5. Answer: C) They should be genuine and specific

Rapport Building Cheatsheet

Objectives:

- To build effective strategies for building rapport with anyone
- To establish trust and prepare the soil of their mind for more profound and engaging conversations

Introduction:

Building rapport is the genesis of all connections. It creates an atmosphere of trust and understanding in just a few minutes. Without preparing the soil of someone's mind, you cannot engage in deeper conversations. By using the strategies presented in this chapter, you can build rapport with anyone and move from talking about the "WHAT" to the "WHO" behind the "WHAT."

Two Methods of Building Rapport:

1. Look for Commonalities and Ask an Open-Ended Question

- Draw attention to something you have in common, such as a shared interest
- Begin with small talk and the ability to find common ground to build trust
- Transition from small talk to deep talk by asking an open-ended question about that commonality
- Demonstrate an interest in the speaker's point of view by asking an open-ended question after pointing out a commonality

Example Scenario: You notice someone with a book from your favorite author at a coffee shop

- Commonality: "Hey, I noticed your book, and I love the author's work."
- Example Question: "What's your favorite book by the author?"

2. Give a Compliment and Ask Open-Ended Questions

- Compliments are a great way to start a conversation and build relationships because they are full of positive energy
- Compliments must be genuine and specific
- Compliment them on their personality, energy, mindset, and other less obvious characteristics
- Follow up with an open-ended question

Example Scenario: You meet a new colleague and want to establish a good relationship

- Compliment: "I admire your attention to detail in your work."
- Example Question: "How did you develop your skill for detail-oriented work?"

Tips:

- Be genuine and specific with your compliments
- Listen actively and ask open-ended questions
- Avoid talking only about the "WHAT," and instead, transition to the "WHO" behind the "WHAT" for more profound and engaging conversations.

Worksheet: Building Rapport (Preparing the Soil)

Objective: To reinforce the learning from Chapter 3 on building rapport and provide readers with a practical tool to apply the strategies in their daily interactions.

Instructions:

1. Refer to Your Rapport-Building Cheatsheet:

- Look at the "Rapport-Building Cheatsheet" you received or created earlier in the chapter.
- Use it as a reference and reminder of the key strategies, tips, and examples discussed in the chapter.

2. Identify and document commonalities:

Instructions: Identify commonalities with a few people in your group and write them down. Next, generate open-ended questions to initiate deeper conversations based on those commonalities. Write your answers in the provided spaces.

Person 1:

Commonalities:

1. ______________________________
2. ______________________________
3. ______________________________

Open-Ended Questions:
1. ____________________
2. ____________________
3. ____________________

Person 2:

Commonalities:
1. ____________________
2. ____________________
3. ____________________

Open-Ended Questions:
1. ____________________
2. ____________________
3. ____________________

Person 3:

Commonalities:
1. ____________________
2. ____________________
3. ____________________

Open-Ended Questions:
1. ____________________
2. ____________________
3. ____________________

3. Brainstorm Compliments and Follow-up Questions:

Instructions:

- Reflect on the importance of giving genuine and specific compliments in building rapport.
- Brainstorm a list of compliments you can give others in your group.
- Next to each compliment, write down a follow-up open-ended question that can lead to a more in-depth conversation.

Compliments and Follow-up Questions:

1. ____________________
2. ____________________
3. ____________________
4. ____________________
5. ____________________
6. ____________________
7. ____________________
8. ____________________

4. Group Role-Play Practice:

- Pair up with another participant in the workshop or group setting.
- Take turns being the initiator and the responder.
- Use the commonality and compliment strategies to start conversations and practice engaging in deeper dialogue.
- Focus on active listening, asking open-ended questions, and building connections.
- After each role-play practice, provide feedback and insights to each other.

5. Group Discussion and Sharing:

- Gather as a group and share your experiences, challenges, and successes in applying the rapport-building strategies.
- Discuss any aha moments, lessons learned, or tips you found particularly helpful.
- Engage in open dialogue to learn from each other's experiences and gain new perspectives.

6. Individual Application and Reflection:

Outside of the workshop or group setting, actively apply the rapport-building strategies in your daily interactions. Take note of the outcomes, impacts, and improvements you observe in your conversations. Use your workbook to jot down real-life examples of successful rapport-building moments.

7. Review and Revisit:

Regularly revisit the rapport-building strategies in your workbook. Reflect on your progress, revise strategies if necessary, and add new insights about your experiences.

8. Celebrate Your Growth:

As you progress in building rapport, celebrate your achievements and their positive impact on your relationships and interactions.

Remember, building rapport is a skill that comes with practice. Use this workbook activity to reinforce your learning and apply the strategies in your daily life.

Chapter 4: Engaging Questions

Planting Quality Seeds In The Conversation

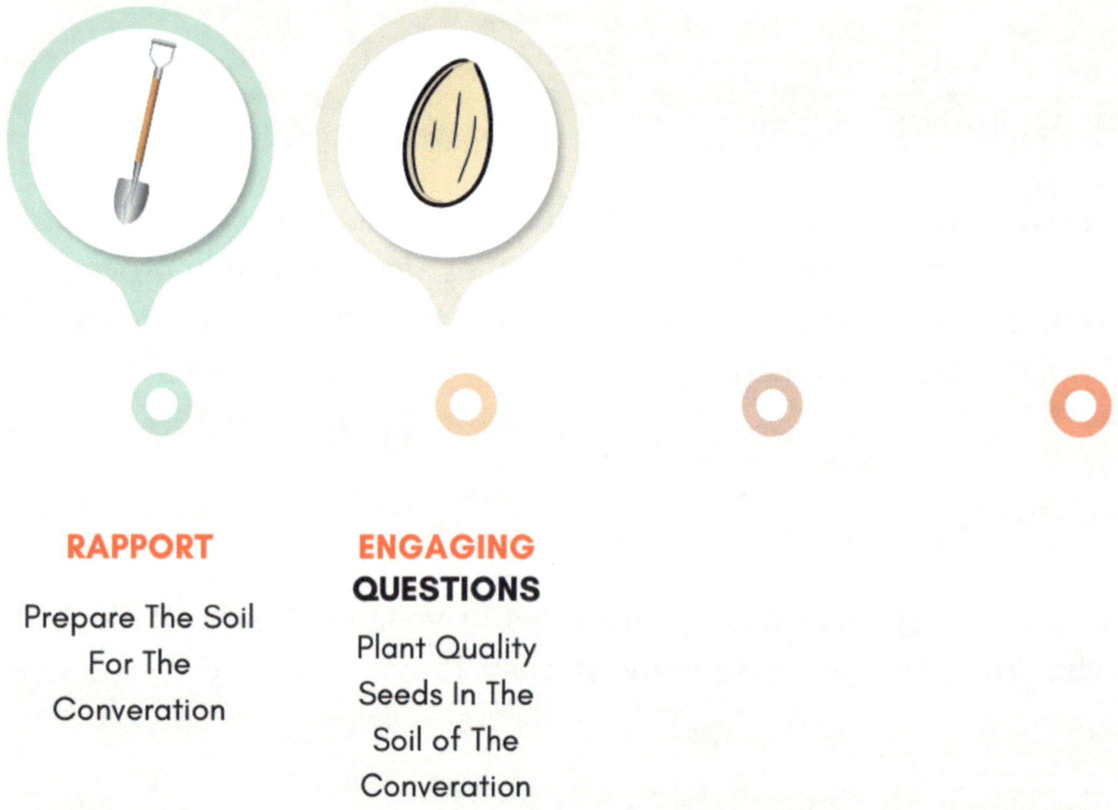

In the previous chapter, we had a great discussion about the first step of the REAP Conversation Method: building rapport. It's like preparing the soil of someone's mind before planting intentional seeds in the conversation. Engaging questions are the second step in this method. These questions give you the ability to navigate towards the intention you desire to see happen in your conversation with someone. It's just like planting seeds for a harvest. If you want the outcome of a watermelon, you wouldn't plant the seed of an apple while expecting the harvest

of a watermelon. But some of us are not cognizant of the questions we ask and how we ask them in order to get the harvest we're looking for from our intentions, and then we end up feeling disappointed, frustrated, and upset. I understand that maybe the person wasn't as cooperative as you thought they would have been in the conversation, but the question is: did you ask an engaging question or an open-ended question? Engaging questions are all about getting to the heart of the matter. They're the ones that make you stop and think, or perhaps even catch you by surprise.

The Difference Between Open-Ended and Engaging Questions:

Have you ever been in a conversation where the exchanged questions could have brought more depth or meaningful dialogue? Maybe the questions focused on simple facts or generic information, lacking the power to ignite engaging and insightful responses. These types of questions are mistaken for open-ended ones, but they are closed-ended ones that limit conversation flow. Engaging questions, on the other hand, go beyond surface-level information and aim to elicit vivid descriptions, personal experiences, and emotions from the respondent.

For example, let's compare these two questions:

1. What are your favorite foods?
2. When you were a kid, what were your favorite foods that your parents fixed?

Both questions are technically open-ended, but the second question transports the conversation to a specific time and place, prompting the person to recall childhood memories and share more detailed and meaningful information. The essence of an engaging question is that it invites the person to go deeper and contribute to a richer conversation.

Characteristics of Engaging Questions:

Engaging questions are the backbone of meaningful conversations. They have specific characteristics that set them apart and make them powerful tools for building rapport and deeper connections.

Here are the characteristics of engaging questions:

1. Intentionality:
The first characteristic of engaging questions is intentionality. When asking engaging questions, it's important to have a clear purpose in mind. What do you hope to learn or explore through the question? By being intentional with your questions, you can guide the conversation meaningfully and create a more engaging environment.

2. Help Paint a Vivid Picture:
Engaging questions encourage the person to describe a scene, experience, or emotion in detail. They use vivid language and imagery to create a mental picture that transports the listener and enriches the conversation.

For instance, instead of asking, "Did you enjoy your vacation?"

An engaging question could be, "Can you describe the most breathtaking view you encountered and how it made you feel?"

This question invites the person to paint a vivid picture with their words, allowing for a more engaging and immersive conversation.

3. Evoke Emotions:
Engaging questions to tap into the person's emotions and feelings. They go beyond simple factual information and encourage individuals to share their experiences and their associated emotions.

For example, instead of asking, "What movies do you like?" an engaging question could be, "What was the last movie you watched that made you feel emotionally connected to it?" This question invites the person to reflect on the emotional impact of a particular movie, leading to a deeper and more meaningful discussion.

4. Provide Relevant Context:

Engaging questions are specific to the subject and the respondent. They demonstrate active listening and a genuine interest in the other person's thoughts and experiences. By providing relevant context, you show you are attentive and engaged in the conversation. They help create a more meaningful and personalized dialogue. For instance, if you are discussing a recent trip, instead of asking a generic question like, "Did you have a good time?" you can ask, "What was the most memorable experience you had during your trip, and why did it leave such an impact on you?" This question considers the conversation's context and allows for a more engaging discussion.

5. Refer to Specific Timeframes:

Engaging questions have the ability to tap into specific timeframes, such as past experiences or future aspirations. By narrowing the focus, you provide the person with a clear frame of reference, making it easier for them to respond and share their thoughts.

Here are a few examples to illustrate how specific timeframes can enhance the power of engaging questions:

Past Experiences: When discussing a general topic, like "memorable vacations," you can make it more specific by asking, "Tell me about the most unforgettable vacation you had in the past year." By setting a specific time frame, you prompt them to recall recent experiences and share a story that is fresh in their memory.

Nostalgic Moments: If you want to explore nostalgic memories, you can ask something like, "What was your favorite childhood toy or game before the age of 10?" This question focuses on a specific time frame in their early years, prompting them to revisit their childhood memories and share meaningful anecdotes.

College Years: To delve into college experiences, you might ask, "What was the most significant event or accomplishment during your sophomore year?" By pinpointing a specific year, you help them reflect on a particular time period and encourage them to share a specific story or experience from their college life.

The power of engaging questions that use specific timeframes lies in their ability to prompt individuals to relive memories and gain new insights about their past experiences. As they share these stories with you, they may even discover different perspectives and lessons learned that relate to their current lives. The beauty of it all is that these positive feelings will be associated with you as the person who asked a specific enough question to evoke such reflective storytelling.

Incorporating these characteristics into your questions allows you to plant quality seeds in conversations and nurture them into fruitful exchanges. Engaging questions are powerful tools for building rapport, fostering connection, and creating meaningful conversation.

Building Rapport + Engaging Questions

To further understand the essence of engaging questions and how they they work with building rapport first, let's explore some examples:

1. Commonality + Open-Ended Question + Engaging Question:

Initiating rapport building: "I heard you played basketball in high school. That's great! I was a shooting guard for my high school basketball team.

Open-Ended Question: "Which position did you play?"

Engaging question: "That's awesome! Basketball coaches often have valuable insights and advice. Is there any specific advice from your coaches that you still remember and apply today?

Engaging Question characteristics:

- specific advice from your coaches = Refer to Specific Timeframes/help paint a picture
- remembering and applying in your life today = Evoke Emotion

2. Genuine Compliment + Open Ended Question + Engaging Question:

Initiating rapport building: "Your work on that project was impressive. How did you come up with such a unique approach?"

Engaging question: "What was the most challenging part of the project, and how did you overcome it?

Engaging characteristics:

Most challenging = evoke emotions.

How did you overcome it? = Help paint a vivid picture.

With those two examples, you can clearly see how rapport and engaging questions go hand in hand. When building rapport, you start by using open-ended questions to initiate a connection and create a comfortable atmosphere. Then, as the conversation progresses, you transition to engaging questions that dive deeper beyond the surface.

Remember, asking engaging questions creates an environment where the other person feels comfortable sharing and expressing themselves. By reflecting on your intention, encouraging sharing, creating emotional connections, staying relevant, and reframing when necessary, you can elevate your conversations to a deeper and more meaningful level.

The R2E Rule:

The R2E Rule (Relation to Exploration) empowers conversations and fosters a deeper level of engagement. This powerful questioning technique holds value in professional environments, where the establishment of trust and the promotion of open communication can prove challenging due to past negative experiences or existing mistrust. By implementing the R2E Rule, individuals can overcome these barriers and cultivate a communication dynamic that is more positive and productive.

The R2E Rule involves relating to a topic or experience before asking an open-ended question that encourages exploration and sharing. This technique establishes a personal connection and demonstrates your willingness to be vulnerable and open. It creates a safe space for others to open up and share their thoughts and experiences. One of the best aspects of this technique is that you can ask deeper and more personal questions without feeling like you're being too invasive, which will spark mistrust and skepticism from past experiences.

When should I use the R2E Rule?

In order to effectively use the R2E Rule (Relation to Exploration), it's important to prepare the soil of someone's mind by building rapport in the introduction phase. Understanding the phases of conversation and recognizing opportune moments to employ the R2E Rule can enhance your communication skills.

Let's explore these phases and how the R2E Rule fits in:

1. Opening/Introduction Phase:

During this initial stage, individuals establish rapport and engage in small talk. It creates a comfortable atmosphere and fosters a sense of connection and trust. By implementing the strategies and utilizing the tools provided in the building rapport chapter, you will swiftly progress to the next phase.

2. Transition Phase:

As the conversation moves beyond superficial topics, you can introduce the R2E Rule. By relating your experiences or thoughts (relation) to the ongoing conversation, you continue to build rapport and show genuine interest. This transition encourages the other person to open up and leads to a more meaningful and engaged discussion.

Here's an example:

Relation: "I've always been fascinated by travel. I recently took a trip to Italy and fell in love with the culture and cuisine.

Exploration: What travel experiences have left a lasting impression on you?"

3. **Exploration Phase:**

During this phase, integrate the relational aspect of the R2E Rule before asking an exploration question. By sharing a personal experience, insight, or reflection related to the topic (relation), you further solidify the rapport you've established. This sets the stage for a more meaningful and engaged discussion. Remember, the R2E has to be related to the topic at hand so that it is not used randomly without any connection to the conversation.

Example:

Relation: "When I faced a challenging project deadline last year, I had to develop effective time management strategies to meet the goal. It made me realize the importance of prioritization and breaking tasks into smaller, manageable steps."

Exploration: "Have you ever encountered a similar situation where you had to manage competing priorities and tight deadlines? How did you approach it, and what strategies worked for you?"

4. Closing/Resolution Phase:

The R2E Rule may not play a significant role in this phase as it focuses on summarizing key points, reaching resolutions, or expressing final thoughts. The primary goal is to provide closure and wrap up the conversation. You have to know when to let the conversation go. Knowing when to gracefully conclude a conversation is like nailing the punchline of a joke—timing is everything. In the next chapter, we'll discuss more about how to exit a conversation gracefully, ensuring both parties feel validated.

Remember, by building rapport in the introduction phase, you prepare the soil of someone's mind for the deeper conversations facilitated by the R2E Rule.

Here are a few examples to illustrate the R2E Rule:

1. Relation: "I recently attended a leadership seminar where we discussed the importance of effective communication in teams. It made me reflect on my communication style and the areas I want to improve."

Exploration: "How do you approach communication within your team, and what strategies have you found effective?"

2. Relation: "I've been exploring different strategies to enhance my productivity at work, such as time-blocking and prioritizing tasks. It has been a game-changer for me."

Exploration: "How do you manage your workload and ensure optimal productivity in your role?"

3. Relation: "I recently read a book on personal development that emphasized the power of goal-setting. It inspired me to set clear goals for my career and personal life."

Exploration: "What goals have you set for yourself, and how do you stay motivated to achieve them?"

The R2E Rule allows you to create a deeper level of engagement by establishing a personal connection and inviting others to share their experiences and perspectives. It shows genuine interest in the other person and encourages a meaningful and insightful conversation.

Remember, vulnerability is a crucial aspect of practicing the R2E Rule effectively. Engaging in a healthy inner conversation with yourself and embracing vulnerability empowers you to relate to others and create meaningful connections authentically.

So, embrace vulnerability, engage in a healthy internal conversation, and let it empower you to ask engaging questions that deepen relationships and create meaningful conversations through the R2E Rule.

Let's put your knowledge to work:

I've created three levels of engaging questions, ranging from beginner to advanced to expert. I'll provide you with resources to know the difference.

Now let's put everything we've learned into practice. Building on the rapport-building activity from the previous chapter, we'll create engaging questions that elicit meaningful and in-depth responses. This exercise will help you develop the skill of crafting questions that truly engage others and foster insightful conversations.

Are you ready? Let's get started.

Practicing R2E (Relation to Exploration) Questions

Instructions:

1. Read the example R2E questions at the top of the worksheet.
2. Understand the structure of an R2E question, where you first relate to the topic or experience before asking an open-ended question.
3. Take the five simple questions below and transform them into R2E questions by relating to the topic and asking an open-ended question that explores the other person's thoughts and experiences.
4. Write your R2E questions in the spaces provided.

Example R2E Questions:

1. Relation: "I've been exploring different ways to improve my time management skills, and I've found that creating a daily to-do list has been helpful. It helps me stay organized and focused throughout the day."

Exploration: "What strategies or tools do you use to manage your time effectively?"

2. Relation: "Recently, I've been experimenting with new healthy recipes in the kitchen. One recipe I tried was a quinoa salad with fresh vegetables, which turned out delicious! It made me realize the importance of incorporating nutritious meals into my daily routine."

Exploration: "What are some of your favorite healthy recipes that you enjoy preparing and why?"

Transform the following simple questions into R2E questions:

1. Simple Question: "What hobbies do you have?"

R2E Question:

____

____

2. Simple Question: "Have you ever traveled to another country?"

R2E Question:

____

____

3. Simple Question: "What is your favorite book?"

R2E Question:

____

____

4. Simple Question: "Do you enjoy outdoor activities?"

R2E Question:

____

____

5. Simple Question: "What do you like to do in your free time?"

R2E Question:

____

____

Reflect on your experience of transforming simple questions into R2E questions and consider how this technique can help deepen your conversations and build rapport with others.

Sharing R2E Questions

Instructions:

1. Reflect on the R2E Rule (Relation to Exploration) example provided above and familiarize yourself with the concept.
2. Find a partner you haven't worked with yet for this exercise.
3. Take a moment to introduce yourselves and briefly get to know each other through the rapport techniques.
4. Using the R2E Rule, create engaging questions that build upon the connection you established with your partner during the previous activities. Remember to incorporate the relational and exploration components into your questions.
5. Aim to create at least two R2E questions based on the commonalities or compliments you identified with your partner in step 3.
6. Write down your R2E questions in the spaces below.

R2E Question 1:
Compliment/ Commonality:

____

____

Open Ended Question:

____

Relation:

Exploration:

R2E Question 2:
Compliment/ Commonality:

Open Ended Question:

Relation:

Exploration:

7. Once you have crafted your R2E questions, take turns asking them to your partner. Engage in deeper conversations based on your questions and actively listen to each other's responses.

8. Show genuine interest in your partner's experiences and ask follow-up questions to explore the topic further.

9. Reflect on the impact of using the R2E Rule in your conversation. Did it help create a more open and comfortable atmosphere for sharing? Did it lead to deeper insights and meaningful dialogue?

10. Take note of any lessons or insights you gained from this exercise and consider how to incorporate the R2E Rule into future conversations to foster stronger connections and collaboration.

Remember, the R2E Rule is powerful for building rapport and fostering open communication. By relating your experiences and inviting others to explore their own, you create a safe and engaging environment for meaningful conversations to thrive. Practice and refine your R2E questioning skills, and you'll be well on your way to cultivating engaging and productive discussions with your partner.

Key Phrases to Make Questions More Engaging

1. Help Paint a Vivid Picture:

- Can you describe in detail...
- Tell me how...
- Share with me what it looked/smelled/sounded like...
- Walk me through the process of...
- Paint a picture of the moment when...
- Help me visualize what it was like...

2. Evoke Emotions:

- How did it make you feel when...
- What emotions did you experience while...
- Can you recall a time when you felt...
- Describe a moment that evoked strong emotions like...
- Share an experience that deeply touched you emotionally...

3. Provide Relevant Context:

- Based on what we've been discussing...
- Considering your expertise in...
- In relation to our previous conversation about...
- Building upon what you mentioned earlier...
- With your experience in...

4. Refer to Specific Timeframes:

- In the past [timeframe], what stands out as...
- Looking back on the last [timeframe], can you recall...
- Reflecting on [specific event or period], tell me about...

- Considering the future, what are your aspirations for...
- Projecting ahead [timeframe], what do you envision for…
- When you were in [timeframe], what was the best…

Beginner-Level Engaging Questions (1 Characteristic Used)

Think of beginner-level, engaging questions as the seeds you sow in the conversation soil. These seeds are tiny and straightforward, like the humble beginnings of a conversation. They hold the potential for growth and connection, just like seeds sprouting into plants. As you plant these questions, you lay the foundation for deeper interactions, nurturing the growth of meaningful conversations.

1. "When you think about your favorite childhood memory, can you vividly paint a picture of the scene [Help Paint a Vivid Picture]?"

2. "What movie or book has had such a powerful emotional impact on you [Evoke Emotions] that it still resonates with you today?

3. "In our discussion about personal growth, can you provide an example from your life that illustrates how a specific experience or challenge has shaped your perspective [Provide Relevant Context] or approach?"

4. "Can you recall a significant milestone or achievement from the past year [Refer to Specific Timeframes] and describe how it has influenced your goals and aspirations moving forward?"

Please note that the highlighted sections within each question indicate the specific characteristics of engaging questions.

Advanced-Level Engaging Questions (2 Characteristics Used)

Transitioning to advanced-level, engaging questions is like planting more diverse and robust seeds in your conversation garden. These seeds are selected with a deeper understanding of the characteristics you want to cultivate. They possess the potential to yield more engaging and insightful conversations. Like different seeds that grow into distinct plants, these questions offer a greater variety of topics, emotions, and perspectives, allowing conversations to flourish in unique ways.

1. When [a specific event or circumstance] occurred in your life, what uncomfortable emotions did you experience?
   (Combines "Refer to Specific Timeframes" and "Evoke Emotions")

2. What have been two of your most effective rituals or habits this past year that have led to a healthier mindset and personal growth?
   (Combines "Help Paint a Vivid Picture" and "Refer to Specific Timeframes")

3. When you faced restructuring the entire sales department last year, how did you maintain a positive mindset to take phenomenal action steps to overcome the obstacles along the way?
   (Combines "Refer to Specific Timeframes" and "Provide Relevant Context")

These questions provide an example for creating advanced-level, engaging questions based on your experiences and insights.

Expert-Level Engaging Questions (3 or More Characteristics Used)

Expert-level, engaging questions are your conversation garden's rare and exceptional seeds. They are the seeds of profound connection and transformation. These seeds are carefully curated to represent a deep understanding of the art of conversation. Just as rare and exotic seeds produce extraordinary plants, these questions can ignite memorable conversations that touch people's hearts and minds. They foster deep empathy, exploration of emotions, and a genuine exchange of ideas.

1. Last summer, during your backpacking trip through the mountains, what breathtaking moment filled you with a sense of awe and wonder, evoking a deep connection to nature, and how did that experience shape your perspective on the world?

   (Highlights "Help Paint a Vivid Picture" - vividly describing the breathtaking moment, "Evoke Emotions" - evoking a sense of awe and wonder, and "Provide Relevant Context" - referring to a specific time last summer)

2. When reflecting on your most cherished holiday memories from childhood, which specific tradition or family gathering still brings intense nostalgia, warmth, and joy? How do those emotions impact your present-day celebrations and connections with loved ones?

   (Highlights "Evoke Emotions" - intense feelings of nostalgia, warmth, and joy, "Provide Relevant Context" - referring to childhood holiday memories, and "Refer to Specific Timeframes" - reflecting on past experiences)

3. During the challenging project you undertook in the spring of 2022, what significant milestone or accomplishment not only filled you with a sense of pride and fulfillment but also brought forth a deep understanding of your personal growth, resilience, and potential for future success?

(Highlights "Provide Relevant Context" - referring to a challenging project in the spring of 2022, "Refer to Specific Timeframes" - specifying the time frame, and "Evoke Emotions" - evoking a sense of pride, fulfillment, personal growth, resilience, and potential)

Now it's your turn to create engaging questions.

Transforming Questions - From Basic to Expert Engaging

Instructions:

In this assignment, you can practice transforming questions from basic open-ended to expert-level engaging questions. Engaging questions foster deeper conversations and establish a stronger connection with others. Applying the characteristics we discussed will elevate the quality of your questions and enhance your communication skills.

1. Beginner-Level Transformation:

Transform the following basic open-ended question into a beginner-level engaging question by incorporating one characteristic, such as helping paint a vivid picture or evoking emotions:

- Basic Question: "What do you enjoy doing in your free time?"
- Beginner Level Engaging Question:

____

____

2. Advanced-Level Transformation:

Take your beginner-level engaging question from step 1 and elevate it to an advanced level by incorporating two characteristics, such as providing relevant context and referring to specific timeframes:

- Beginner Level Engaging Question:

____

____

- Advanced Level Engaging Question:

____

____

3. Expert-Level Transformation:

For the final part of the assignment, elevate your advanced-level engaging question to an expert level by incorporating three or more characteristics, such as helping paint a vivid picture, evoking emotions, providing relevant context, and referring to specific timeframes:

- Advanced Level Engaging Question:

____

____

- Expert Level Engaging Question:

____

____

____

Remember to consider the characteristics of engaging questions as you transform them from basic to expert level. This assignment will help you enhance your questioning skills and develop the ability to create meaningful and impactful conversations.

Engaging Questions Practice Worksheet

Instructions for Engaging Question Practice with a New Partner:

1. Find a new partner for this activity. Look for someone you have yet to pair up with.

2. Decide who will be Partner 1 and Partner 2.

3. Partner 1: Share a commonality or compliment Partner 2 to establish a connection that creates context.

Commonality/Genuine Compliment: [Write your commonality or genuine compliment here]

Commonality/Compliment:____

Open-Ended Question:____

4. Partner 1: Reflect on the commonality or compliment and develop an engaging question that builds upon it. Consider incorporating the characteristics of engaging questions, such as vivid imagery, emotional impact, relevant context, or specific timeframes.

Partner 1 Engaging Question

____

____

5. Partner 2: Listen attentively to Partner 1's engaging question and respond thoughtfully. Then, create an engaging question that builds upon the rapport and extends the conversation. Use the characteristics of engaging questions to make your question more immersive and meaningful.

Partner 2 Engaging Question

____

____

6. Take turns asking each other the engaging questions you wrote, ensuring that each question builds upon the rapport and previous responses.

Partner 1:

Rapport(Commonality or Compliment + Open Ended Question):

Commonality/Compliment:______________________________

Open-Ended Question:______________________________

Engaging Question: [Ask your engaging question here]

____

____

Partner 2: Respond thoughtfully.

Partner 2:

Commonality/Compliment:______________________________

Open-Ended Question:______________________________

Engaging Question: [Ask your engaging question here]

___

___

Partner 1: Respond thoughtfully.

7. Reflect on your experience as you engage in the conversation. Consider how the engaging questions impact the depth and meaningfulness of the interaction.

- **Reflection Questions:**

  - How did answering engaging questions affect the conversation?
  - Did it lead to a deeper and more meaningful interaction?

8. Take notes throughout the activity to capture insights or learnings for future reference.

Additional Notes:

- Pairing up with a new partner allows you to build connections with different individuals.
- Be fully present and actively listen to your partner's responses to create an engaging and genuine conversation.
- Enjoy exploring new perspectives, sharing experiences, and building a stronger connection with your partner.

Conclusion:

Congratulations on completing the Engaging Questions chapter! You've mastered crafting thought-provoking questions that create deeper connections and meaningful conversations. It's like planting seeds of curiosity and watching them grow into fruitful interactions.

Throughout this chapter, we've explored the characteristics of engaging questions, from painting vivid pictures to evoking emotions, providing relevant context, and referring to specific timeframes. These characteristics can transform conversations and create a safe space for authentic sharing.

And let's not forget the R2E Rule (Relation to Exploration), a game-changing technique that takes your conversations to a whole new level. By sharing your experiences before asking open-ended questions, you foster trust and invite others to explore their thoughts and experiences.

It's important to remember that intention plays an essential role in asking engaging questions. Your questions become even more powerful when you approach a conversation with genuine curiosity and a desire to connect. So, as you continue your journey, infuse your questions with intention and see the magic unfold.

As we transition to the next chapter, get ready to dive into the world of active listening, the third step of the REAP Method. Like watering seeds in a garden, active listening nourishes the conversations you've started with engaging questions, allowing them to flourish and bear fruitful results.

In the upcoming chapter, we'll explore the importance of attentive and focused listening, uncovering techniques to understand and empathize with others. Prepare to cultivate meaningful connections through the power of active listening.

Remember, engaging questions and active listening go hand in hand to create fruitful conversations. So, let's continue our journey and unlock the potential of active listening to foster more profound understanding and meaningful conversation.

Chapter 5: Active Listening

Water the Seed of Conversation & Watch It Grow

We have laid the groundwork by using your skills to build rapport. Then, by asking engaging questions, we planted the seeds for this conversation, which is now leading you to the results you intended before you began the conversation. Now it's time to water the seed you've sown. Just like a plant needs water to grow and thrive, your conversation requires active listening as its source of nourishment.

Surprisingly, although the majority of people claim to be good listeners, it's rare to find individuals who truly take the time to listen to each other when they interact.

We often find ourselves distracted by other pressing issues or preoccupied with our thoughts on what to say next. Showing respect and giving our full attention to others is a challenging skill to master, but it's a necessary one to watch the fruit you desire for your conversation begin manifesting itself.

I always say that if you're not listening to me, you're not respecting me. The first law of love and respect is to listen. Reflect on your own experiences to confirm this. Think back to when you were conversing with someone who constantly interrupted or seemed mentally absent, more focused on what they wanted to say than being fully present with you. If we genuinely want to establish lasting connections, we must be willing to listen attentively and empathetically.

The truth is, though, that while you think someone is listening to you, not all listeners are the same. There are some people who are passive listeners. Passive listeners simply hear without any further engagement. They allow someone to express themselves without interruption, but they lack true connection and understanding. You might get a lazy response from them like "that's cool" or "that's amazing" or "sorry to hear that," or let me not leave out the fan favorite "that crazy."

On the other hand, active listening involves responding to the speaker's words to show an understanding of their intended message. It goes beyond the common non-focused or passive listening we often engage in during everyday conversations.

One of the remarkable powers of active listening is creating a safe and open space for the speaker to express themselves more deeply and reach new levels of understanding. However, active listening is not an easy skill to master. It requires deliberate action, honed listening skills, dedicated effort, focused attention, and consistent practice.

So, what is the significance of active listening?

Imagine if you're genuinely committed to growing the fruits you desire and planting a wonderful seed in the ground, nurtured by the rapport you've built. But what if you neglect to water that seed? It will wither and die. Active listening is the water that nourishes your conversations and allows them to flourish. It's a learnable skill that nourishes the other person's thoughts and emotions and gives them a sense of security and well-being. As they begin to share more of themselves, the fruits of your relationship will bear sweet results. Remember, the fruits of your conversations grow through active listening, not just passive listening or sharing your point of view. That's why active listening holds such great importance.

Why is Listening Challenging?

Now, let's explore why listening has become increasingly challenging today.

1. **Multitasking:** Research suggests that multitasking can lead to decreased productivity and performance. A study conducted at Stanford University found that individuals who frequently engage in multitasking tend to have more difficulty filtering out irrelevant information and focusing their attention, which affects their ability to listen attentively in conversations.

2. **Information overload:** According to a report by the Nielsen Norman Group, excessive information overload can result in decreased comprehension, decreased memory retention, and reduced attention span. The constant influx of notifications and information from various digital platforms can overwhelm our cognitive capacity, making it challenging to maintain sustained attention during conversations.

3. **Time constraints:** Modern life's fast-paced nature, busy schedules, and time pressures can limit the time we allocate for meaningful conversations. A study published in the Journal of Applied Psychology found that time pressure can hinder the quality of

communication and reduce individuals' ability to engage in active listening behaviors.

4. **Personal biases and assumptions:** Research has shown that personal biases and assumptions can impede effective communication and listening. A study published in the Journal of Personality and Social Psychology found that individuals with preconceived, solid beliefs tend to engage in more selective listening, filtering out information that contradicts their views and limiting their ability to listen deeply and understand different perspectives.

While these observations provide insights into the potential impact of multitasking, information overload, time constraints, and personal biases on active listening and attentiveness, it's important to note that individual experiences may vary. But if we neglect to water the seeds we've planted by not cultivating our listening skills, we will never find the fruits we seek. Our scattered thoughts prevent us from truly listening to others clearly and attentively.

Ah, active listening—an essential step in the process of creating fruitful conversations. It's part of the REAP Conversation Method that requires our utmost attention and effort.

You see, we humans are wired to communicate and express ourselves. Our natural inclination is to jump in and share our own opinions and thoughts. But active listening? Well, that's a whole different ballgame. It requires us to put aside our inner chatter, resist distractions, and be present in the conversation.

How often do we mentally drift off or think about what we want to say next? It's common. We are bombarded with stimuli, from phone notifications to the never-ending to-do lists in our minds. It's no wonder that active listening can feel like a challenge.

But here's the beauty of it: when we master the art of active listening, we unlock a world of possibilities. We become the nurturers of the person we engage with, creating a safe space for them to grow and blossom. Through active listening, we witness the transformation as their ideas take shape and their perspectives deepen.

Imagine having a conversation where the other person feels honestly heard and understood. You can set the trend for that in your organization, on your team, and in your personal life.

So, let's roll up our sleeves and dive into active listening. We'll explore practical strategies and techniques to enhance our listening skills. We'll learn to silence our inner chatter, resist the pull of distractions, and, indeed, be present with those we engage with.

Remember, becoming a better active listener may not be easy. It takes practice, patience, and a genuine willingness to grow.

The Stages of Active Listening

Understanding and applying the stages of active listening is the foundation for becoming an exceptional listener. Let's look at each stage and explore how you can effectively engage in active listening to enhance your communication skills and build meaningful connections.

1. **Receiving:** The first stage of active listening is receiving. It involves fully attending to and hearing the information. To effectively receive the speaker's message, minimize distractions and focus your attention on their words. Create a conducive environment that lets you be fully present in the conversation. Practice silence and avoid interrupting the speaker, giving them the space to express themselves without interruption. Utilize attentive body language, such as maintaining eye contact, leaning in, and using facial expressions or head nods to show your engagement.

2. **Understanding:** Once you have received the speaker's message, the next stage is understanding, which involves assigning meaning to the message and interpreting the speaker's intent. Take the time to process the information and comprehend the underlying message. During this stage, you can demonstrate understanding by paraphrasing or summarizing the speaker's words. For example, you might say, "If I understood correctly, you're saying that..." You'll be showing the speaker that you are actively listening and trying to grasp their perspective. Asking clarifying questions is another effective way to deepen your understanding and ensure you correctly interpret their message.

3. **Remembering:** After understanding the speaker's message, retaining the information in your memory is important. Remembering involves actively storing the details and key points shared during the conversation. One helpful technique is taking notes and jotting down important ideas or keywords that will aid your recall later. Additionally, connect the speaker's message with your existing knowledge or experiences, which will help you remember the information and enable you to engage in a more meaningful and relevant conversation.

4. **Evaluating:** In the fourth stage of active listening, you evaluate the speaker's message, which involves critically assessing the information received. Consider the content, context, and relevance of the message. Evaluate the validity, accuracy, and reliability of the information shared. It is important to approach this stage with an open mind and suspend judgment. Avoid making assumptions or jumping to conclusions prematurely. By adopting a curious mindset, you can ask thoughtful questions to explore the speaker's ideas and perspectives further.

5. **Responding:** Active listening goes beyond simply understanding and evaluating; it requires responding to the speaker. Responding involves giving feedback to demonstrate your understanding and create a meaningful dialogue. Show that you have actively listened by paraphrasing, summarizing, or asking clarifying questions. For example, you might say, "So, if I understood correctly, you're feeling..." or "Let me make sure I've got this right." You confirm your comprehension and encourage the speaker to provide more information or elaborate on their thoughts.

Now, it's important to note that we will delve deeper into effective ways to respond in our next chapter, so hang tight. We will explore various techniques and strategies to foster effective communication and maintain the flow of conversation.

Active Listening Skills In Different Contexts

Active Listening Skills in Person:

- Practice silence and attentive body language, such as maintaining eye contact and using affirmative gestures like head nods. You'll show your engagement, encouraging the speaker to continue sharing.

- Lean in slightly to show your interest and attentiveness. This physical gesture conveys that you actively listen and focus on the conversation.

- Let go of random thoughts and distractions, allowing yourself to be fully present in the interaction. Avoid mentally formulating responses while the speaker is talking; give them your undivided attention.

Active Listening Skills on the Phone:

- Set a timeframe and mentally prepare for the call.

You can minimize distractions and be fully present by allocating dedicated time for the conversation.

- Remove all applications from your screen to reduce the temptation to multitask and maintain your focus on the conversation.
- Turn off the TV or any other background noise that may divert your attention. Create a quiet and focused environment to facilitate active listening.
- Avoid interrupting the speaker and allow them to finish their thoughts before responding. Practice patience and let the conversation flow naturally.
- Follow the flow of the conversation and stay focused. Avoid getting sidetracked or letting your mind wander. Maintain active engagement by actively listening and responding appropriately.

Incorporating these active listening skills into your personal and professional interactions allows you to foster stronger connections, gain a deeper understanding of others, and navigate conversations with empathy and respect. Stay tuned for the next chapter, where we'll delve into practical ways to respond and keep the conversation flowing smoothly.

But before we get there, let's test your active listening knowledge and skills.

End of Chapter Quiz:

1. Which of the following is not one of the five stages of active listening?

A. Receiving
B. Understanding
C. Evaluating
D. Responding
E. Analyzing

2. Why is active listening important?

A. It conveys respect to others and creates a space for deeper understanding and connection
B. It allows you to control the conversation and steer it in the direction you want
C. It helps you develop clever responses to impress others
D. It shows that you are in charge and have authority over the conversation

3. What is the difference between passive and active listening?

A. Passive listening is non-reactionary and does not provide feedback or ask questions, while active listening responds to the speaker's words and reveals their intended feelings.
B. Passive listening is always better than active listening.
C. Active listening involves nodding your head and smiling, while passive listening involves ignoring the speaker.
D. Passive listening is the same as daydreaming, while active listening is the same as taking notes.

4. Which of the following is a characteristic of effective active listening in person?

A. Checking your phone for notifications during the conversation
B. Interrupting the speaker to share your thoughts
C. Practicing silence and attentive body language
D. Focusing on unrelated thoughts instead of the conversation

5. Which of the following is a strategy for effective active listening on the phone?

A. Setting a timeframe and mentally preparing for call
B. Turning on the TV to watch while you talk
C. Interrupting the speaker frequently to ask questions
D. All of the above

Answer Key:

1. Which of the following is NOT one of the 5 stages of active listening?
Answer: E

2. Why is active listening important?
Answer: A

3. What is the difference between passive and active listening?
Answer: A

4. Which of the following is a characteristic of effective active listening in person?
Answer: C

5. Which of the following is a strategy for effective active listening on the phone?
Answer: A

Active Listening Skills Cheat Sheet

Active listening is a skill that can help you better understand and connect with others. Follow these tips to practice active listening:

Receiving: Hear the communicated message.

- Focus your attention on the speaker and minimize distractions.
- Listen for the sounds, tone, and content of the message.

Understanding: Interpret the message and its context.

- Ask questions to clarify the message and show your interest. For example, you could ask, "Could you provide more details about that?"
- Paraphrase what you've heard to show you understand. You can say, "If I understood correctly, you're saying..."

Remembering: Retain the information for future use.

- Pay attention to details and key points. Take note of important facts or ideas.
- If necessary, jot down brief notes to help you remember the key points later.

Evaluating: Assess the information received.

- Assess the message's validity and determine its importance. Consider the speaker's credibility and the relevance of the information.
- Reflect on the speaker's goals and motivations. Try to understand their perspective and underlying intentions.

Responding: Give feedback to the speaker.

- Summarize the speaker's message to demonstrate your understanding. You can say, "So, if I understood correctly, you're saying..."
- Ask questions to show interest and deepen your understanding. For example, you could ask, "How did you come to that conclusion?"
- Provide feedback and offer suggestions respectfully and constructively. Share your thoughts while considering the speaker's feelings and maintaining a collaborative tone.

In-Person Listening Tips:

- Practice silence and attentive body language. Avoid interrupting the speaker and give them space to express their thoughts.
- Lean in and utilize facial expressions and head nods to show your engagement and encouragement.
- Let go of random thoughts and distractions and focus on the conversation's flow.

Over-the-Phone Listening Tips:

- Set a timeframe and mentally prepare for the call. Create a dedicated space and time to focus solely on the conversation.
- Remove all applications from your screen to minimize distractions. Give your full attention to the conversation.
- Turn off the TV and other potential sources of distraction to maintain focus.
- Avoid interrupting the speaker and allow them to finish their thoughts before responding.
- Follow the flow of conversation and stay focused on the speaker's words.

Active Listening Activity

Building Conversation through Rapport-Building and Active Listening

Part 1: Building Rapport

Pair up with a new partner and take turns finding a commonality or giving a genuine compliment.

Commonality/Genuine Compliment: [Write your commonality or genuine compliment here]

Commonality/Compliment:____

Open-Ended Question:____

Part 2: Engaging with Active Listening and Engaging Questions

Practice the five stages of active listening while your partner shares their chosen topic.

Ask an engaging question that not only builds upon the rapport but also incorporates the four characteristics of engaging questions discussed earlier:

- Helps paint a picture
- Evokes an emotion
- Is contextual
- Has a specific timeframe

Engaging Question: [Write your engaging question here, incorporating the characteristics]

____

____

____

Practice active listening again while your partner responds to your engaging question.

Part 3: Reflection

Reflect on your experience:

After your partner has finished sharing their topic, ask them to rate your listening skills using the Active Listening Rating sheet provided.

- They will rate the statements based on how often they observed your listening behavior during the conversation.
- Take a moment to reflect on your listening skills based on the ratings given by your partner.
- Consider the areas where you received lower scores and ask your partner how you can improve your listening skills in those specific areas.
- Engage in a follow-up conversation with your partner, focusing on their responses to your engaging questions.
- Practice active listening as they respond, showing genuine interest and understanding.

Active Listening Rating Sheet

Instructions:

- After completing Part 2 of the Active Listening Activity Sheet, ask your partner to rate your listening skills based on the statements provided.
- They will rate each statement based on how often they observe your listening behavior when speaking to you.
- Ask them to circle the number that best describes their perception.
- After rating each statement, add the scores based on the circled numbers for each statement.

Circle the number that best describes your partner's behavior.

Statement	Often	Sometimes	Seldom	Never
Finds listening to others uninteresting	4	3	2	1
Tends to focus attention on the speaker's delivery and appearance	4	3	2	1
Listens more for facts and details, often missing the points that give facteaning	4	3	2	1
Easily distracted by other people talking, chewing gum, rattling paper, and so on	4	3	2	1
Fakes attention, looking at the speaker but thinking about other things	4	3	2	1

Statement	Often	Sometimes	Seldom	Never
Listens only to what is easy to understand	4	3	2	1
Certain emotional laden words interfere with their listening	4	3	2	1
As they hear a few sentences about another person's problems, they immediately start thinking about all the advice they can give	4	3	2	1
Attention span is very short, so they can't listen for more than a few minutes	4	3	2	1
Quickly find things to disagree with, so they stop listening as they prepare for an argument	4	3	2	1
Tries to appease the speaker by being supportive through head-nodding and uttering agreement, but not involved	4	3	2	1
Will change the subject when they get bored or uncomfortable with it	4	3	2	1
As soon as someone says anything they think reflects negatively on them, they jump in to defend themselves	4	3	2	1
Second guesses the speaker, trying to figure out what they really mean	4	3	2	1
Directs the conversation back to themselves	4	3	2	1

Add the scores based on the circled numbers for each statement.

Interpretation:

- **15-24:** The person you spoke to has good listening skills overall, but they can still improve in some areas.
- **25-34:** The person you spoke to has okay listening skills. They have some skills to be a good listener, but there's more to learn.
- **35-44:** The person you spoke to has fair listening skills. However, they still have quite a lot of skills to master.
- **45-54:** The person you spoke to can use improvement on their listening skills. It's difficult for them to listen to others, and their messages are often misunderstood.
- **55+:** The person you spoke to needs to work on their listening skills. It's challenging to communicate with them, and they often misunderstand the messages being conveyed.

Embracing Proper Response Tools

As we conclude this chapter on active listening, we continue our journey of tending to the seed of conversation. By applying these active listening skills, we provide the nourishing water that helps the seed grow and flourish. And now it's time to bring out our Proper Response Tools.

Proper Response Tools are the tools we use to harvest the fruit of fruitful conversations, responding in a way that fosters understanding and growth. These tools empower us to craft thoughtful and impactful responses that further deepen the connection and propel the conversation forward. They enable us to navigate the twists and turns of dialogue with finesse and grace.

Just as a skilled farmer knows which tool to use for each stage of the harvest, we too can learn to wield the Proper Response Tools effectively. From asking probing questions to providing insightful reflections, these tools allow us to shape the conversation and create a space for mutual understanding and growth.

Chapter 6: Proper Responses

Harvest The Fruit of Your Conversations

RAPPORT

Prepare The Soil For The Converation

ENGAGING QUESTIONS

Plant Quality Seeds In The Soil of The Converation

ACTIVE LISTENING

Water The Seed & Watch It Grow

PROPER RESPONSE

Go and harvest the fruit you've grown with the right tools.

As we reflect on our journey through the REAP Conversation Method, it becomes abundantly clear that the success of our conversations hinges on our ability to respond properly. Like a skilled harvester who can gather the ripest fruits without causing harm, our responses must be precise and nurturing. Without the right tools and techniques, our well-intentioned words may inadvertently damage the fruits we have carefully cultivated.

Throughout this journey, we have explored building rapport, engaging connections, and actively listening to others. We have witnessed the fruits of our efforts, seeing conversations flourish and relationships deepen. However, to fully savor the rewards of our labor, we must now focus on the "P" stage of the REAP Conversation Method: "properly responding."

In the realm of work, let's acknowledge the challenges associated with ineffective communication. According to a Gallup survey conducted in 2017, 70% of employees reported leaving a job because of a bad manager. This exodus can be attributed, at least in part, to the inability of these managers to respond properly to their team members' needs. Similarly, a 2018 study by OfficeVibe revealed that 65% of employees have received negative feedback that lacked constructiveness. Such feedback, rather than inspiring growth and improvement, can lead to disengagement and dissatisfaction. Additionally, a 2019 LinkedIn survey found that over half of employees (55%) have felt ignored or unappreciated in the workplace, emphasizing the detrimental impact of inadequate responses.

To counteract these negative outcomes, it's imperative to embrace the power of validation in our responses. By incorporating validation, we create a safe and supportive environment where individuals feel heard, understood, and valued. When someone shares their experiences, thoughts, or emotions, validation assures them that their words matter and that their contributions are acknowledged. This simple validation can alleviate tensions, build trust, and deepen connections, ultimately fostering a more positive and productive work environment.

In our pursuit of fruitful conversations, we must remember the importance of validation in every response.

What is Validation?

Validation isn't about agreeing, placating, repeating what someone said, or trying to change someone. It's about letting the person know "your feelings and thoughts, even if I don't understand them at the moment, are important to me."

It's letting that person know, "Our connection matters."

The Need For Validation

If someone is sharing precious aspects of their life, it is imperative to create space for them mentally and skillfully to handle what they are saying to deepen that connection. When responding outside of the 4 proper response tools, disconnection is inevitable.

PART 1: KNOW, FEEL & EXPERIENCE

Conversations start with questions, hopefully engaging ones, or by responding to what someone has done.

When these two things happen, people will share 3 things:

- What they know.
- What they feel about something.
- What they have experienced.

Based upon what they did or shared, you will think or feel several ways, including

- Agreement
- Relatability

- Disagreement
- Offended
- Confused
- Inquisitive to learn more about...
- Conflicted
- Surprised
- The need to provide a solution and more…

VALIDATING BEFORE RESPONDING

With regard to what you're feeling from their actions or response, here are some things to note before responding:

Have the self-awareness to know if you're listening and understanding through the lens of unprocessed trauma, also known as trauma filters, which we discussed earlier. That will determine how you feel about what's being said, what someone did, and how you'll respond. If you feel offended or triggered, there's a way to handle this matter properly. Be sure the reason you're triggered is not only by what they said but also by what you haven't processed within your inner conversation. This is why I stressed exploring your inner conversation before striving to apply this method, because this method is built upon the foundation of healthy communication practices that must start within first.

ALWAYS VALIDATE BEFORE RESPONDING

This is a crucial thing to remember before responding. I can't say this loud enough! When you validate before responding, even when feeling offended, this will provide so much understanding. You'll be able to salvage the conversation, gain clarity, and strengthen the connections. How does validation sound when responding?

Here's a quick cheat sheet of validating statements to be used in every conversation.

Validation Response Cheat Sheet

- I love that/how you...
- I love it when you...
- I appreciate you (insert action you appreciate) ...
- You stated that very well.
- You provided me with great insight on...
- Your feeling of (insert emotion) is understandable.
- I feel you on that.
- It makes sense that you feel...
- It makes sense that you think...
- I am sorry you feel that way. What happened? (Don't ask what's wrong)
- Thank you for...
- It means a lot to me that...
- I value your ability to...
- I didn't know I made you feel that way when...
- You having an (emotion shared) day is understandable based on what you shared with me.

The 4 Proper Response Tools

Now that we have discussed what validation is, why it's important, and how it sounds, it's time to dive into the proper 4 ways to respond in any conversation with your person of interest so that you can continually deepen your connection.

In this chapter, I will show you how to always validate before using the proper response tools.

Get ready to deepen your relationships with these response tools.

1. Validation to Exploration

Validation to Exploration is a powerful tool that involves validating what someone has done or said to you and then following up with a thoughtful question. It helps create a safe and open space for the person to express themselves without feeling interrogated, judged, or dismissed. By validating their actions, words, or feelings, you show that you genuinely value their perspective and are interested in understanding them better.

Let's explore some example scenarios where validation to exploration are applied:

1. Disagreement:

You find yourself in a conversation where you hold a different opinion from the other person. Instead of immediately expressing your disagreement, you first validate their viewpoint. For example, you might say, "I appreciate your perspective on this matter. It's clear that you've put a lot of thought into it. Can you help me understand why you see it that way?" (Validation: "I appreciate your perspective on this matter." Exploration: "Can you help me understand why you see it that way?")

2. Perplexity:

The person you're talking to shares something confusing or puzzling. Instead of dismissing their statement, you validate their experience and seek further clarification.

You might respond with, "That's an interesting point. I'm not quite sure I follow. Could you provide more context or examples to help me grasp what you mean?" (Validation: "That's an interesting point." Exploration: "Could you provide more context or examples to help me grasp what you mean?")

3. Curiosity:

You feel intrigued by what the person is sharing, even if it challenges your beliefs or experiences. Rather than shutting down the conversation or imposing your assumptions, you validate their thoughts and express your curiosity.

For instance, you could say, "I find your perspective fascinating. I'd love to learn more about how you arrived at this viewpoint. Could you share some of the experiences or insights that led you to think this way?" (Validation: "I find your perspective fascinating." Exploration: "Could you share some of the experiences or insights that led you to think this way?")

4. Providing Solutions:

The person expresses a problem or challenge they're facing, and you have some ideas or suggestions. Instead of immediately jumping in with your solutions, you validate their feelings and ask if they're open to exploring potential solutions together. You might respond with, "I can sense that you're feeling frustrated by this situation. Would you be interested in brainstorming some possible approaches? I'm here to support you." (Validation: "I can sense that you're feeling frustrated by this situation." Exploration: "Would you be interested in brainstorming some possible approaches?"

Incorporating validation into exploration in these scenarios creates a space for genuine dialogue, understanding, and connection. Remember, the goal is to show empathy, curiosity, and respect, allowing the conversation to unfold organically and collaboratively.

The Validation to Exploration response tool works wonders. It safeguards the growth of the conversation and deepens the connection by gaining more insight into what the other person is saying. This powerful method prevents uncomfortable thoughts or negative responses from disconnecting the conversation.

This tool will help you harvest the rich fruits of your relationships through conversation. Get ready to unlock new levels of communication and connection!

2. Validation to Relation

Validation to Relation is a response type that involves first validating what someone has shared with you and then relating to their experience. It's a natural inclination for us to empathize and connect with others when their words resonate with our experiences. However, handling this response type is crucial to avoid hijacking the conversation and making the other person feel unheard.

Here are some key points to remember when using Validation to Relation in conversation:

Fully Listen: Practice discipline and understand the other person's experience before interjecting with statements like, "Me too!" or "That happened to me as well!" or "I did the same thing!" Let them have their moment to share without interruption.

Validate First: Prioritize validating what they've shared before attempting to relate to it. It's essential for them to feel heard and understood by you before you share your own experiences.

Ask to Relate: You might wonder why asking for permission to share your experience is necessary. Well, there are a couple of reasons. Firstly, sharing your experience can provide a solution, but someone might not need it now. Secondly, asking for permission allows the person to be a willing listener to your experience, fostering a mutual exchange.

So how does Validation to Relation sound? First, let's explore how it doesn't sound.

How Validation to Relation Does Not Sound:

You asked: "What lessons did you learn from your first job that have helped you?"

They answered: "My very first job was as a lifeguard, and I learned the importance of staying alert and being responsible for others' safety."

Incorrect Response: "Oh, I can relate! I worked as a cashier and had to be responsible for handling money and providing good customer service."

In this example, the response doesn't fully validate the person's experience and quickly shifts the focus to a different job without a solid connection to lifeguarding.

How Validation to Relation Sounds:

You asked: "What lessons did you learn from your first job that have helped you?"

They answered: "My very first job was as a lifeguard, and I learned the importance of staying alert and being responsible for others' safety."

Validating Statement: "That's fantastic! It's incredible how being a lifeguard teaches you the value of vigilance and responsibility for others' well-being."

Ask to relate: "May I share a similar experience?"

Proceed to relate and share your experience.

Correct Response: "May I share a similar experience? I also had a job where I had to prioritize the safety and well-being of others. I worked as a camp counselor, and being responsible for a group of kids taught me the importance of staying vigilant and ensuring their safety at all times."

In this example, the response starts with a validating statement acknowledging and appreciating the person's insight. Then, it seeks permission to relate to their experience and shares a relevant and relatable personal experience.

So, the next time you find an opportunity to relate to someone's experience, remember to validate, seek permission, and explore through follow-up questions. Embrace this proper response tool, and watch your connections deepen and flourish in ways you never thought possible. Get ready to harvest the rich fruits of meaningful conversation using Validation to Relation.

3. Validation to Summarization

What is Validation to Summarization?

Validation to Summarization is a response tool that involves validating and summarizing the key points someone has shared. It guarantees that the essence of the person you are conversing with is fully understood. This method is handy when you don't have a follow-up question or a personal experience to relate to what was shared. It's a perfect tool to gracefully exit a conversation while ensuring the other person feels safe, heard, and understood before you part ways.

For example:

How Validation to Summarization does not sound like this:

Scenario 1: When you have to go:

You asked: "Tell me about your recent hiking trip. What was the most challenging part?"

They answered: "The most challenging part was climbing a steep, rocky trail. It required a lot of endurance and strength, but the feeling of accomplishment at the summit was incredible."

Incorrect Response: "That sounds tough. I'm happy you had a good trip. Alright, I have to head out now. Catch you later!"

In this scenario, the response lacks validation and summarization. It acknowledges the information shared but does not demonstrate understanding or appreciation for the person's experience. Moreover, it abruptly ends the conversation without leaving the other person feeling heard or valued.

Scenario 2: Movie Release

You asked: "What are your thoughts on the latest movie release?"

They answered: "I haven't watched it yet, but I heard it received mixed reviews. Some people loved the storyline, while others thought it lacked depth."

Incorrect Response: "Oh, I've seen it already and loved it! The storyline was captivating, and the acting was superb. You should watch it!"

In this scenario, the response immediately shifts the focus to your own experience without validating or summarizing what the person said. It dismisses their viewpoint and imposes your opinion on them, potentially shutting down further conversation.

How does Validation to Summarization sound?

Let's explore an example to see how Validation to Summarization works:

Scenario 1: When you have to leave:

You asked: "Tell me about your recent hiking trip. What was the most challenging part?"

They answered: "The most challenging part was climbing a steep, rocky trail. It required a lot of endurance and strength, but the feeling of accomplishment at the summit was incredible."

Correct Response: "Wow, climbing that steep and rocky trail sounds like quite an adventure! I can imagine that it must have required tremendous endurance and strength. The feeling of accomplishment you experienced at the summit must have been truly amazing. I'm so glad you got to experience that. I have to head out now, but it was great talking to you. Let's catch up again soon!"

In this scenario, the response acknowledges and validates the person's experience by highlighting their challenges and their sense of accomplishment. It shows genuine interest and appreciation for their story. It then gracefully communicates the need to end the conversation while expressing a desire to reconnect.

Scenario 2: You asked, "Set the scene for me. What was the best part of the last vacation you took?"

They answered: "The last time I took a vacation was to Puerto Rico. That hotel was amazing! It was right off the water, and I had a large balcony where I could just sit and hear the sound of the water and look at the waves. It was very soothing because I loved being by the water and hearing the sound of the water. Whether running water in the bathroom, being in the shower for a while, etc., that was the best part: just sitting off that balcony and having time to reflect and enjoy that peace. The food was good at different restaurants."

Validation & Summarization: "I love that you enjoyed the hotel in Puerto Rico, especially the balcony where you could hear the peaceful sounds of water while looking at the waves and reflecting. From what you said, being anywhere by the water seems incredibly soothing. Now I understand."

Give a pause for silence for about 3 seconds:

This allows for three options:
for them to continue speaking.
for you to ask a follow-up question.
You gracefully exit the conversation, leaving them feeling heard and validated.

Use Validation to Summarization Today

This is a powerful tool for everyday conversations. Apply it today and see how it enhances your interactions. We're now transitioning to the last, but often overlooked, proper response tool for harvesting good fruit in your relationships.

4. Validation to Sharing

What is Validation to Sharing?

Validation to Sharing is a response tool that involves validating what someone has shared before answering the question they asked you. It ensures their response is acknowledged and appreciated before you share your answer. This tool is handy when someone asks you a question after sharing their thoughts. By using Validation to Sharing, you prevent the other person from feeling conversationally neglected or unheard.

How does Validation to Sharing sound?

Let's explore an example to illustrate the difference:

Traditional Scenario (How Validation to Sharing Does Not Sound):

You asked: "Which seasons of the year make you feel the best?"

They answered: "I love the feeling of fall because of the crisp weather, the ability to dress differently, and because it feels nostalgic. What about you? What season of the year makes you feel best?"

Incorrect Response: "The feeling of the spring does it for me..."

What's wrong with this situation?

In this scenario, their answer about the joys of fall was not validated or acknowledged. It lacked a genuine connection to their response.

Correct Scenario:

You asked: "Which seasons of the year make you feel the best?"

They answered: "I love the feeling of fall because of the crisp weather, the ability to dress differently, and because it feels nostalgic. What about you? What season of the year makes you feel best?"

Validation: "I love that fall brings a sense of nostalgia for you. I completely understand how the change in weather and the opportunity to dress differently can create a unique experience. The outfits in the fall have a different vibe than in the summer, where you don't have to wear as much."

Now, you can answer their question: "The feeling of spring does it for me because..."

Bonus: Transition to Exploration (follow-up question): "What specifically about fall brings that nostalgic feeling to you?"

By applying Validation to Sharing, you ensure the other person's response is acknowledged and valued before sharing your answer. It keeps the conversation flowing and allows for deeper connection and understanding.

Apply Validation to Sharing today and ensure the people you connect with never feel neglected or unheard before you share your answers.

Now it's time to put your knowledge and response skills to the test. But before we put the entire REAP Conversation Method together in the final exam, I'll give you a cheat sheet and some practice on how to properly respond.

Proper Response Cheat Sheet:

Objectives:

- Importance of proper responses in a conversation
- Tools and techniques for proper responses
- Impact of improper responses on the conversation
- Benefits of using proper response tools to deepen connections

Key Points:

- Proper responses require validation
- Validation is not agreement, placation, or repeating to make them feel good
- Know, feel, experience: People usually share what they know, feel, and have experienced in conversations
- Always validate before responding
- The 4 Proper Response Tools: Validation to Exploration, Validation to Relation, Validation to Summarization, and Validation to Sharing

Validation:

- Validates the person's experience and feelings
- Acknowledges and respects another person's experiences and feelings
- Builds trust and deeper connections within conversation

Validation to Exploration:

- Validate what someone has said or done and ask a follow-up question
- Avoids making the person feel like they're being interviewed or interrogated
- Explore any other feeling before assumption

Validation to Relation:

- Validating what someone said before relating to them about your own experience
- Best used when you've had a similar experience that resonates with what they've shared
- Ask for permission to relate and share your own experience

Validation to Summarization:

- Validates and summarizes key parts of the conversation
- Shows active listening and avoids dismissive generic responses
- Provides an opportunity for continuation, follow-up, or graceful exit

Validation to Sharing:

- Validates what someone shared before answering their question
- Used when you ask a question and they respond with a question
- Prevents feelings of conversational neglect
- Validates the person's response before answering their question to deepen the conversation

End of Chapter Quiz:

1. What is the goal of using proper response tools in a conversation?

A) To establish a foundation for the conversation
B) To avoid common conversational pitfalls like misunderstandings and disconnection
C) To deepen the connection and harvest the fruits of the conversation through proper responses
D) To relate to the person's experience before attempting to respond

2. What is the definition of "validation" in a conversation?

A) Agreement, placation, or repeating to make the person feel good
B) Acknowledging and respecting another person's experiences and feelings
C) Repeating what the person said to show you were listening
D) Sharing your own experiences to relate to the person

3. What are the three things people usually share in a conversation?

A) Facts, opinions, and solutions
B) Knowledge, experience, and attitude
C) What they know, what they feel, and what they have experienced
D) Thoughts, feelings, and solutions

4. Why is validation important before responding to someone in a conversation?

A) To show you were listening to what they said
B) To provide clarity and strengthen connections in communication
C) To avoid common conversational pitfalls like misunderstandings and disconnection
D) All of the above

5. What are the four proper response tools in a conversation?

A) Validation, exploration, relation, summarization
B) Agreement, disagreement, offense, confusion
C) Questioning, interrupting, sharing, disagreeing
D) Generic responses, validation, summarization, exploration

6. What is the purpose of using Validation to Exploration in a conversation?

A) To limit unwanted thoughts or responses that could disconnect the conversation
B) To deepen the connection and gain more insight into what the other person is saying
C) To validate what someone said first and then relate to it
D) To validate and summarize key parts of the conversation,

7. How should you use Validation to Relation in a conversation?

A) Listen fully before relating to the person's experience
B) Relate to someone's experience before validating what they've shared
C) Only share your own experience if it's not helpful or necessary
D) Interrupt mid-sentence and take over the conversation

8. What is the purpose of using Validation to Summarization in a conversation?

A) To show active listening and avoid dismissive generic responses
B) To validate the person's response before answering their question
C) To validate what someone shared before answering their question
D) To relate to what someone said first and then summarize it

9. Why is it important to use Validation to Sharing in a conversation?

A) To deepen the connection and gain more insight into what the other person is saying
B) To avoid common conversational pitfalls like misunderstandings and disconnection
C) To prevent the conversation from feeling rushed or forced
D) To validate the person's response before answering their question

Answer Key:

1. C) To deepen the connection and harvest the fruits of the conversation through proper responses
2. B) Acknowledging and respecting another person's experiences and feelings
3. C) What they know, what they feel, and what they have experienced
4. D) All of the above
5. A) Validation, exploration, relation, summarization
6. B) To deepen the connection and gain more insight into what the other person is saying
7. A) Listen fully before relating to the person's experience
8. A) To show active listening and avoid dismissive generic responses
9. D) To validate the person's response before answering their question

Practicing Proper Responses

1. Validation to Exploration

Scenario: Your conversation partner shares their passion for painting and how it brings them joy.

Partner Statement: "I find painting a therapeutic and meditative activity. It allows me to express my emotions and create something beautiful."

Validation: ______________________________

Exploratory Question: ______________________________

2. Validation to Relation

Scenario: Your conversation partner talks about their recent hiking adventure and their challenges.

Partner Statement: "I recently took a challenging mountain hiking trip. The steep trails and unpredictable weather made it physically and mentally demanding."

Validation: ______________________________

Relatable Experience: ____

3. Validation to Summarization

Scenario: Your conversation partner shares their excitement about starting a new business venture.

Partner Statement: "I'm thrilled to embark on this new business venture. After months of planning and preparation, I finally launched my online store. It's a dream come true!"

Validation: ____

Summarization: ____

4. Validation to Sharing

Scenario: Your conversation partner expresses frustration with a difficult work situation.

Partner Statement: "I'm feeling so overwhelmed at work. The constant deadlines and high expectations make maintaining a healthy work-life balance challenging. How is it for you to maintain a work-life balance?"

Validation: ____

Personal Experience/Insight: ____

Putting it All Together:

Now it's time to put it all together. You've come this far in learning how to prepare the soil, plant quality seeds, water the seeds, and see them grow. Now it's time for you to harvest the fruits that have grown from your conversation with the proper response techniques.

Let's put it all together and use the REAP Conversation Method entirely!

Applying The REAP Conversation Method

Instructions:

- Find a new partner and introduce yourself.
- Decide who will be Partner 1 and who will be Partner 2. (Partner 1 will go first.)
- Fill out the sections of the REAP Conversation Method form related to your conversation until the Active Listening stage, as you won't be able to decide your responses in advance.
- Set a timer for 5 minutes. Partner 1 will initiate the conversation and lead for 5 minutes, while Partner 2 actively listens and utilizes proper responses.
- Once the 5 minutes are up, set another timer for 5 minutes.
- Partner 2 will now take the lead and converse with Partner 1, who will actively listen and respond using proper responses.
- After each response you provide in the conversation, take a moment to reflect and write down which proper response types you used in the designated space on the form.
- Finally, your partner will provide feedback on your partner feedback form in the book, rating how effectively you applied the REAP Conversation Method.

1. Build rapport with your partner using either of the following:

A. Look for Commonalities and Ask an Open-Ended Question: Find something you have in common with your partner and ask an open-ended question related to that commonality.

Commonality: ____________________

Open-Ended Question: ____________________

B. Give a Compliment and Ask Open-Ended Questions: Give your partner a genuine compliment and then ask an open-ended question.

Compliment: ____________________

Open-Ended Question: ____________________

2. Ask your partner an engaging question that meets one or more of the following characteristics:

- Help paint a picture
- Evoke an emotion
- Contextual
- Specific Timeframe

3. Engaging Question:

____

____

____

4. Actively listen to your partner while being mindful of the 5 Stages of Active Listening:

1. Receiving
2. Understanding
3. Evaluating
4. Remembering
5. Responding

5. Use one of the proper response types within the context:

- Validation to Exploration
- Validation to Relation
- Validation to Summarization
- Validation to Sharing

Response Type Used:

____

Partner Feedback Worksheet: Applying The REAP Conversation Method

Partner Feedback:

When you finish the conversation, fill out the worksheet below to rate your partner's performance in each category. Your partner will evaluate how you applied the REAP Conversation Method.

Partner's Name: ______________________________

How well did your partner build rapport with you?

a. 1 – Poor
b. 2 – Fair
c. 3 – Good
d. 4 – Very Good
e. 5 – Excellent

Honest Comments:

____

____

____

How engaging was the question your partner asked you?

a. 1 – Poor
b. 2 – Fair
c. 3 – Good
d. 4 – Very Good
e. 5 – Excellent

Honest Comments:

____

____

____

How well did your partner actively listen to you?

a. 1 – Poor
b. 2 – Fair
c. 3 – Good
d. 4 – Very Good
e. 5 – Excellent

Honest Comments:

____

____

____

How well did your partner respond to you using the proper response type?

a. 1 – Poor
b. 2 – Fair
c. 3 – Good
d. 4 – Very Good
e. 5 – Excellent

Honest Comments:

____

____

____

Total up your partner's score:

Building Rapport: ______/5
Engaging Question: ______/5
Active Listening: ______/5
Proper Response: ______/5

Total Score (out of 20): ______

To pass, participants must score at least 70% (14 points out of 20)

Discuss the ratings and score with your partner.

Remember, this exercise aims to improve your communication skills, so use your partner's feedback to identify your strengths and areas for improvement.

Using The REAP Conversation Method In Different Scenarios

Now that you've studied, practiced, and are on your way to mastering how to produce fruitful conversations almost at will, I want to show you some ways you can effectively utilize the REAP Conversation Method. This method applies to various situations, but I'll provide three examples of how you and your team can immediately implement this method within your company. By doing so, you can expect excellent results in high productivity and increased employee engagement. Let's explore how these three scenarios apply to this method, enabling you to enjoy fruitful conversations within your work environment today.

Whether you're a team leader, manager, or experiencing conflict with a colleague, these three scenarios will benefit you.

Don't believe me? Let's take a look at the statistics.

According to a survey by the Society for Human Resource Management (SHRM), 90% of employees consider effective communication important for job satisfaction.

A study by the Aberdeen Group found that companies with high levels of employee engagement are 21% more profitable than those with low levels of engagement.

This exercise observed that 85% of employees experience conflict at work.

The American Psychological Association (APA) also found that 29% of employees have to deal with conflict almost constantly.

These statistics demonstrate the negative impact of communication challenges and conflicts on productivity, stress levels, and employee turnover.

Although those statistics are alarming, I wouldn't have needed them to communicate this because, from my experience alone working within the corporate space as a corporate trainer and peak performance coach, primarily for sales professionals and managers, I have witnessed the truth of this firsthand. My office often became a safe haven for sales professionals seeking to realign their perspectives on matters both inside and outside of the office that were impacting their ability to perform at their best. They were not receiving adequate support from their direct superiors and leaders. Eventually, I was tasked with training managers on how to effectively engage with their teams, but I digress. The moral of the story is that during these meetings and sessions, the consensus was that they were able to return to their positions and perform exceptionally well due to the method I am sharing with you in this book.

Now, let's dive into how you can enhance teamwork dynamics with the REAP Conversation Method. Let's explore some realistic scenarios to see how this method can be applied effectively.

Team Meetings

Scenario: Team Meeting - Project Kickoff

Role: Team Leader

Set Your Intention: As the team leader, I intend to facilitate an effective and productive team meeting where everyone feels heard, valued, and engaged. I want to create an environment that encourages open communication, collaboration, and problem-solving, ultimately leading to better team performance and outcomes.

You are conducting a team meeting with your department to discuss a new project that requires cross-functional collaboration. The goal of the meeting is to align everyone on the project objectives, assign roles and responsibilities, and establish a timeline for deliverables.

Rapport Building:

As the meeting begins, you take a moment to connect with each team member individually. You greet them warmly, ask about their day, and show genuine interest in their well-being. This rapport-building approach helps create a positive and inclusive atmosphere where everyone feels comfortable expressing their ideas and concerns.

Engaging Questions:

To encourage active participation and gather valuable input from the team, you ask engaging questions that stimulate discussion, critical thinking, and creativity.

You start by asking, "How do you envision the result of this project impacting our clients? Paint a picture of success for us." This question encourages team members to think beyond the immediate tasks and consider the ultimate goals and outcomes of the project.

Next, you ask, "What emotions do you associate with taking on this new challenge? How do you feel about the project?" This question taps into their experiences and feelings, allowing them to express their initial impressions and concerns.

To provide contextual understanding, you ask, "How does this project align with our department's long-term goals? How does it contribute to our overall strategy?" This question helps team members see the bigger picture and understand the significance of their work within the broader organizational context.

Lastly, you inquire, "What specific milestones or deliverables do you believe we should achieve within the first month?" This question sets a timeframe and encourages team members to think about the immediate goals and targets for the project.

Active Listening:

As team members start sharing their thoughts, ideas, and concerns, you practice active listening. You maintain eye contact, give a nod to show understanding, and avoid interrupting. By fully receiving and understanding their messages, you demonstrate that their input is valuable and foster an environment of trust and respect.

Proper Responses:

Validation to Exploration:

One team member shares their perspective on the project, highlighting the importance of creative freedom in delivering innovative solutions. You validate their input by acknowledging their valuable contribution. You respond, "Thank you for sharing your insights. You've evidently considered the impact on our clients, and your vision aligns well with our objectives. Could you elaborate further on how you envision their experience changing?"

Validation to Relation:

Another team member expresses concerns about the project's tight timeline, fearing it may compromise quality. You validate their concerns by acknowledging and relating the potential challenges to a similar experience. You say, "I understand your concern about the timeline. We've encountered similar situations, and it's important to address them. Can you share any strategies or ideas based on your previous experience that might help us navigate this timeline effectively?"

Validation to Summarization:

As the discussion progresses, you summarize the key decisions, action points, and timelines to ensure everyone is aligned. You say, "Let's summarize what we've discussed so far. We have identified the project objectives, assigned roles and responsibilities, and established a timeline for deliverables. By the end of this month, we will have completed the initial research phase and be ready to move into the design phase. Does that sound accurate to everyone?"

Validation to Sharing:

Towards the end of the meeting, a team member asks for your insights on a specific aspect of the project. Before sharing your thoughts, you validate their question by acknowledging its relevance and importance.

You respond, "That's a great question. I appreciate your curiosity and attention to detail. Before sharing my insights, let me gather more information from the team and ensure we have considered all perspectives. I'll follow up with you individually to discuss it further."

Applying the REAP conversation method in this team meeting scenario created a collaborative and inclusive environment where team members felt valued and engaged. Through rapport building, asking engaging questions, active listening, and responding with proper techniques, you have fostered open communication, addressed concerns, ensured clarity in roles and responsibilities, set the foundation for a successful project, and enhanced team performance.

Performance Meetings

With underperforming team members

Scenario: Performance Meeting with an Underperforming Team Member

Parties Involved:

- Emily: Team Leader
- Sam: Underperforming Team Member

Set Your Intention: Emily's intention for this performance meeting is to create a supportive and constructive environment where Sam feels comfortable discussing their challenges and receives guidance to improve their performance. She aims to foster growth, provide feedback, and develop an action plan for Sam's development.

Step 1: Rapport Building

Emily: "Sam, I appreciate your dedication to our team and the effort you put into your work. I want to discuss your performance and find ways to support your growth. How do you feel about our working relationship so far?"

Step 2: Engaging Questions

Emily: "Sam, to help us better understand the challenges you're facing, could you provide some insights into what factors you believe are contributing to your underperformance? Is there anything specific that you feel is hindering your ability to meet expectations?"

Step 3: Active Listening

Emily: "Receiving": Emily pays full attention to Sam's explanation, maintaining eye contact and displaying attentive body language.
Emily: "Understanding": Emily seeks clarification to ensure a clear understanding of Sam's challenges and concerns.
Emily: "Evaluating": Emily evaluates the validity of Sam's concerns and identifies areas where support and improvement are needed.

Step 4: Proper Responses

Option 1: Validation to Exploration
Emily: "Sam, I appreciate your openness in sharing your challenges. Let's explore these further to gain a deeper understanding. Can you provide more specific examples of the obstacles you encounter and how they impact your performance? It will help us identify strategies to overcome them together."

Option 2: Validation to Summarization
Emily: "Sam, thank you for sharing your thoughts on the factors contributing to your underperformance. To summarize, it seems that time management and prioritization are areas that require attention. Let's discuss potential strategies and solutions to help you improve your efficiency and meet expectations."

Option 3: Validation to Relation
Emily: "Sam, I understand your struggles. I've encountered similar challenges in the past. Would you mind if I related to you on that? When I faced similar situations, I found that setting clear goals and breaking them down into smaller tasks helped me manage my time better. Can we explore how this approach could work for you?"

Option 4: Validation to Sharing
Emily: "Sam, I appreciate your willingness to share your thoughts and concerns. To answer

your question, one approach that could help create a personalized development plan This plan can outline specific actions, resources, and support that will assist you in addressing the areas of improvement we discussed. What are your thoughts on that?"

By applying the REAP Conversation Method in this performance meeting, Emily creates an environment where Sam feels heard, supported, and valued. Through active listening and proper responses, Emily encourages open communication, identifies challenges, and develops solutions to support Sam's growth and improvement.

As a result of this performance meeting, Sam feels reassured, supported, and motivated to improve their performance. Emily's guidance and the action plan they create together provide a clear path for Sam's development. The continued feedback and support from Emily enable Sam to make progress, grow professionally, and contribute more effectively to the team's success.

This approach helps foster a positive work environment, strengthens the employee-manager relationship, and empowers team members to reach their performance goals.

Resolving Workplace Conflict

Scenario: Conflict Resolution

Parties Involved:

- Alex: Team Leader
- Taylor: Team Member

Conflict: Alex and Taylor have differing opinions on approaching a creative project. Alex believes in prioritizing meeting deadlines, while Taylor emphasizes allowing creative freedom.

Intention: Alex intends to find a resolution that balances creativity and meeting deadlines while ensuring a harmonious working relationship with Taylor.

Step 1: Rapport Building

Alex: "Taylor, I appreciate your commitment to creativity in this project. I also understand the importance of meeting our deadlines. Let's find a solution that addresses both concerns. How can we strike a balance?"

Step 2: Engaging Questions

Alex: "Taylor, can you share more about why creative freedom is crucial to you? I want to understand your perspective and how we can incorporate it into our project."
Taylor: "Well, I believe that allowing creative freedom enables us to produce unique and innovative results. It helps us stand out from our competitors. What are your thoughts on this?"

Step 3: Active Listening

Alex: "Receiving": Alex pays full attention to Taylor's explanation, maintaining eye contact and displaying attentive body language.
Alex: "Understanding": Alex seeks clarification when needed to ensure a clear understanding of Taylor's viewpoint.
Alex: "Evaluating": Alex considers the validity of Taylor's concerns and evaluates their potential impact on the project's success.

Step 4: Proper Responses

Option 1: Validation to Exploration
Alex: "Taylor, I understand your perspective on the importance of creative freedom. We must think outside the box and deliver unique results. Let's explore how we can incorporate creative elements while meeting our deadlines. How do you suggest we strike that balance?"

Option 2: Validation to Summarization
Alex: "Taylor, thank you for sharing your thoughts on the significance of creative freedom. We both agree on the value of standing out from competitors and must find a way to balance creativity and meeting deadlines. How can we move forward with that in mind?"

Option 3: Validation to Sharing
Alex: "Taylor, I appreciate your dedication to creative freedom. We need to consider different perspectives. To address your concerns, I suggest we create a collaborative project plan. We can establish key creative milestones while ensuring we meet the necessary deadlines. How does that sound to you?"

After engaging in an open and constructive dialogue, Alex and Taylor found a resolution that satisfied their concerns. They agreed to create a collaborative project plan incorporating creative freedom while ensuring the project was complete by the deadline.

Alex noticed a positive shift in the team's dynamics as they implemented their new approach. The team members felt empowered to express their creative ideas and that their input was valued. At the same time, they were motivated to work efficiently and meet project milestones.

The project itself began to thrive as a result of this balanced approach. Creative freedom and deadline adherence brought forth innovative solutions within the given timeframe. The team's work caught the attention of stakeholders and received positive feedback, further boosting their confidence and motivation.

Alex and Taylor's conflict resolution resulted in a successful project and strengthened their working relationship. They developed a greater understanding and appreciation for each other's perspectives. This newfound collaboration spilled over into future projects as they continued to apply the lessons learned from their constructive conversation.

Under Alex's leadership, the team embraced a culture of open communication, active listening, and respectful conflict resolution. As a result, they fostered a creative and productive work environment where everyone's contributions were valued and recognized.

By utilizing the REAP Conversation Method, Alex demonstrated the power of effective communication and empathy in resolving conflicts. The positive outcomes extended beyond this situation, shaping a more harmonious and prosperous team dynamic.

REAP Checklist for Workplace Scenarios

1. Situation:

- Is there a specific situation that has prompted this meeting? If so, briefly describe the situation.
- If the situation has caused any negative emotions, take a moment to process and address them using the 4A Process outlined in "The Best Conversation You Had With Yourself" to ensure you approach the meeting with the right intentions, engagement, and listening mindset.

2. Intention:

- What is your intention for this meeting? What do you aim to achieve?
- Write down your intended outcome for the meeting to keep it in focus throughout.

3. REAP Application: Reaping the Fruits of Effective Communication

Building Rapport:

- Create a supportive and constructive environment.
- Identify commonalities or find genuine compliments to establish rapport.
- Write down how you plan to build rapport with the team members.

Engaging Questions:

- Ask questions that help paint a picture, evoke emotions, provide context, or focus on a specific timeframe.
- Jot down the engaging questions you plan to ask during the meeting.
- Note any specific questions you have for particular team members.

Active Listening:

- Practice active listening techniques outlined in Chapter 5 of the book.
- Be fully present, receive, understand, evaluate, remember, and respond effectively.

Proper Responses:

- Use proper response techniques to foster effective communication.
- Validations to Exploration: Delve deeper into a topic or challenge.
- Validation to Relation: Relate personal experiences to connect and empathize.
- Validation to Summarization: Summarize key points to ensure clarity and alignment.
- Validation to Sharing: Share insights, resources, or strategies to support the team.

You will improve your team meetings, performance meetings, and conflict resolution by using this checklist, and you will create a more productive and collaborative environment. Remember to review your checklist after the meeting to assess your application of the REAP Conversation Method and identify areas for improvement.

Conclusion

Effective communication is the cornerstone of successful relationships, whether they are personal or professional. Through conversation, we connect, understand, and collaborate with others, leading to mutual growth and satisfaction.

In this book, we have explored the REAP Conversation Method as a powerful tool for cultivating fruitful conversations and nurturing meaningful relationships.

Throughout our journey, we have explored into the four steps of this method: Rapport Building, Engaging Questions, Active Listening, and Proper Responses. By mastering these steps, we have equipped ourselves with the skills to create a positive and impactful communication experience.

Building rapport establishes a foundation of trust and understanding, setting the stage for open and authentic dialogue. Engaging questions ignite curiosity and encourage deep exploration, unlocking valuable insights and perspectives.

Active listening allows us to connect with others, fostering empathy and building stronger connections. And by providing proper responses, we validate, relate, summarize, and share, ensuring our conversations are productive and meaningful.

In closing, I emphasize that the power of fruitful conversations lies within every one of us. By embracing the REAP Conversation Method and committing to ongoing practice and self-reflection, we can transform our relationships, boost productivity, and foster a culture of understanding and collaboration.

Please take what you have learned in this book and apply it in your everyday interactions. Let this method guide you toward more fruitful and rewarding conversations in your personal relationships, professional endeavors, or community engagements. Let us create a world where effective communication is the norm and meaningful connections flourish.

Thank you for joining me on this journey, and I wish you all the best in your ongoing pursuit of fruitful conversations.

About The Author

Meet Darius Brown, author of "The Best Conversation You Ever Had Workbook" and your trusted Conversation Coach.

Darius's journey began in the corporate world, where he trained sales professionals on how to communicate effectively with clients and achieve sales targets. However, he soon realized that his true passion lay in helping people apply these communication skills to their personal lives. Darius started breaking down conversational principles and sales techniques in a way that his trainees could apply to their everyday interactions in response to the transformative power of meaningful conversations. The results were astonishing, with trainees reporting improved personal relationships, conflict resolution, and a deeper understanding of their loved ones.

Recognizing the impact of personal challenges on sales performance, Darius bridged the gap by incorporating inner conversations and personal growth into his training programs. By helping sales professionals navigate their inner challenges, he empowered them to cultivate a positive mindset, build resilience, and enhance their overall performance in sales conversations.

Darius's comprehensive coaching programs, developed as valuable employee benefits, have garnered acclaim from a diverse clientele, including famous celebrities, C-suite executives, and high-performing sales teams. However, his focus remains on putting the individual at the center of his work, guiding them through the 4A Process and REAP conversation method to unlock their full potential and create deeper, more fulfilling relationships both at work and at home.

As your Conversation Coach, Darius is dedicated to your personal transformation and the art of extraordinary conversations. His multiple books on having better conversations with yourself and others serve as invaluable resources for personal growth and connection. With Darius by your side, you can navigate your inner conversations, embrace personal growth, and cultivate authentic relationships that make a lasting impact.

Additional Resources

"The Best Conversation You Ever Had With Yourself":
Embark on a transformative journey towards self-mastery with "The Best Conversation You Ever Had With Yourself." This book introduces the 4A Process, guiding you to master your inner conversation and unlock a new level of self-awareness, personal growth, and fulfillment. Discover the power of meaningful self-talk and unleash your true potential.

Conversational Anxiety:
Take control of your conversations and overcome anxiety with "Conversational Anxiety." This book provides practical strategies and tools to help you navigate and conquer listening and sharing anxiety. Learn how to establish healthy boundaries, honor your own needs and emotions, and foster connections that feel freeing, connecting, vulnerable, and intentional.

You Hired Them Now What?
Discover the ultimate guide to team building with "You Hired Them Now What?: 34 Conversation Activities To Build Rapport & Connection With Your New Team." Your Conversation Coach, Darius Brown presents 34 powerful activities to ignite motivation, enhance collaboration, and create a high-performing team.

These books, along with other valuable resources, can be found on our website at www.getyourconversationcoach.com/store

I believe in the power of continuous learning and personal growth, and these resources will support you in developing effective communication skills and navigating the complexities of conversations.

Visit my website today to explore these books and embark on a journey towards empowering and fulfilling conversations.

Keep In Touch!

We would love to hear from you! If you have any feedback, testimonials, or stories about how this book has impacted your team, please feel free to reach out to us at booking@getyourconversationcoach.com

We value your input and appreciate the opportunity to learn more about how this book has made a difference in your team's success. Please share with us any changes you've noticed in your team's key performance indicators (KPIs) from the time you started using this book in your team building meetings until now. Your feedback will help us continue to improve and better serve our readers.

Thank you for your support!

Sincerely,
Your Conversation Coach, **Darius Brown**

Connect with me on LinkedIn

LinkedIn

Made in the USA
Columbia, SC
22 October 2023

24534799R00078